D0597914

29 minutes to dinner

If you have ever wished it was easier to put a quick and delicious meal on the table, this cookbook is for you. The Pampered Chef® Test Kitchens have created an entire collection of quick, easy and smart dinnertime solutions to get you in and out of *your* kitchen in 29 minutes or less—start to finish. Our simple but impressive recipes are packed with flavor as well as time-saving tips, tools and techniques that will inspire you to make homemade meals more often. Whether you're cooking for two or for the entire family, you'll find that preparing a weeknight or weekend meal is easier and more delicious than you ever thought it could be. So gather your ingredients and tools, gather your loved ones around the table, and get ready to enjoy dinner together. It's just 29 minutes away!

Enjoy!

The Pampered Chef® Test Kitchens

On the front cover (clockwise from left): *Brown Butter Tortellini with Spinach & Ham*, p. 87; *Mediterranean Quesadillas with Antipasto Relish*, p. 39; *Barbecue Salmon with Radish Slaw*, p. 65. On the back cover: *BLT Mac & Cheese*, p. 75.

CONTENTS

8 poultry

Versatile and family-pleasing, poultry is the "go-to" meat that is a natural choice when schedules are tight. Our collection of chicken and turkey dishes will expand your recipe repertoire with fast, flavorful and unique dishes that you can depend on when you're on the go.

42 fish & seafood

Toss out the frozen fish sticks; the catch of the day is quick and fresh! We've infused our seafood recipes with plenty of flavor and variety so you're never at a loss for speedy ways to prepare fish that the whole family will enjoy.

68 beef & pork

Beef and pork may evoke images of slow-cooked Sunday roasts and stews, but both can easily fit into a busy lifestyle. The wonderful thing about these meats is that they deliver big flavor in a short amount of time when prepared correctly. Our innovative recipes and techniques will show you how.

100 meatless

For lighter fare, turn to the refreshing, simple recipes in this chapter. Featuring fresh vegetables as well as egg, grain and bean selections, these recipes are satisfying, nourishing and easy ways to add variety to your dinnertime regime.

STEPS TO SUCCESS

1 plan ahead

- Set aside a little time once a week to plan for the week ahead. Choose your recipes accordingly, and shop for perishables and any specialty ingredients that you will need for your recipes.

- This is also a good time to quickly check your stock of staples in the pantry, refrigerator or freezer and replenish what is running low.

2 read the recipe

- Read the recipe from start to finish before beginning. This will allow you to visualize the steps of the recipe.

- Each recipe details the flow of preparation that is done simultaneously. For example, recipes will state when to chop vegetables while rice is cooking or meat is browning.

3 gather the ingredients & equipment

4 start cooking!

- Look over the ingredient list, gather the ingredients you will need and place on your work surface.

- As you read the recipe steps, gather the equipment needed for preparation, cooking and serving.

QUICK COOKING STRATEGIES

Purchase rotisserie chickens or turkey breasts—remove the skin, dice or shred the meat and use in recipes such as *Chicken Posole Verde* (p. 37).

Get potatoes started in the microwave to pare down the overall cook time, as seen in *Artichoke Chicken with Roasted Potatoes* (p. 15).

Cut foods into smaller, evenly sized pieces to cook faster and more evenly, such as in *Almond Chicken Stir-Fry* (p. 33).

Cook foods side by side in the same vessel. This technique is convenient and saves time in clean-up, such as in *Dijon-Crusted Halibut and Roasted Asparagus* (p. 51).

These tips are just a few examples of cooking techniques used in this cookbook that will save you time. For additional ideas on how to shave even more time off of your recipe preparation, see Beat the Clock (p. 124).

- Begin cooking the component of the recipe that takes the longest first. This is usually the meat or the starch.

- If a recipe calls for an ingredient to be used in two different places, such as chopped cilantro in a sauce and as a garnish, chop all of it at once, and set aside part of it for later use.

- Use quick-cooking starches such as couscous and orzo, which are real time savers to round out your meals.

- Pound meats such as chicken breasts to an even thickness. This will allow them to cook quickly and evenly.

- "Doctoring up" jarred pasta sauces with additional herbs, garlic and broth is a great short-cut to homemade flavor in recipes like *Campanelle with Creamy Tomato-Clam Sauce* (p. 67).

- Cooking bell peppers in the microwave for *Spanish-Style Stuffed Peppers* (p. 103) brings out their natural sweetness while cutting down on preparation time.

MORE FLAVOR IN LESS TIME

Cook pasta directly in broth or sauce rather than water to impart more flavor, such as in *BLT Mac & Cheese* (p. 75).

Add small amounts of sugar to enhance flavors and promote browning in recipes like *Shrimp Orzo Skillet* (p. 61).

Add interesting spices, such as in *Paprika Chicken & Egg Noodles* (p. 17) and *Garam Masala Salmon* (p. 57) to give foods authentic flavors.

Choose flavor-packed ingredients like lemon zest, garlic, chipotle peppers, red curry paste, fresh or dried herbs and stronger-flavored cheeses such as Asiago.

The recipes in this book are filled with great ways to add flavor to your recipes when there's little time.

- Make use of the endless varieties of jarred salsas, such as in the recipe for *Tex-Mex Chicken & Rice Skillet* (p. 31) to add zip to recipes in no time.

- Caramelize tomato paste, as seen in *Italian Meatball Soup* (p. 97), which brings out a depth of flavor in just minutes.

- Toast spices and nuts to release their natural oils and crisp them up, making them delicious additions to salads or other dishes.

- Brown foods well to add richness to pan sauces. Deglazing with wine or reducing vinegar adds complexity.

- Store jarred olives and capers in the pantry for whenever a recipe needs an extra kick. Both ingredients are featured in *Moroccan Pork Chops* (p. 99).

- Roast foods at high temperatures or finish them under the broiler for deep, caramelized flavor.

- Thai curry paste instantly provides authentic flavor and heat to any Asian recipe, such as *Hot & Sour Soup* (p. 107). If kept refrigerated, it will last several months without losing flavor. It usually consists of garlic, shallots, turmeric, galangal (aromatic ginger), kaffir lime leaves, hot chilies, lemon grass, coriander, cumin and sometimes shrimp paste.

poultry

Glazed Chicken with Apple Salad, p. 29

PROVENÇAL CHICKEN WITH BROWN RICE

Caramelizing the tomato paste gives this sauce a "slow-cooked" flavor.

RICE

- 1 tsp (5 mL) olive oil
- 1 cup (250 mL) uncooked instant brown rice
- 1 cup (250 mL) chicken broth

CHICKEN

- 1 tbsp (15 mL) olive oil
- 2 boneless, skinless chicken breasts (4-6 oz/125-175 g each)
- 1/4 tsp (1 mL) salt
- 1/8 tsp (0.5 mL) coarsely ground black pepper

SAUCE

- 2 tbsp (30 mL) tomato paste
- 3/4 cup (175 mL) water
- 1 garlic clove, pressed
- 1/4 cup (50 mL) pitted green olives
- 2 plum tomatoes

1. For rice, add oil to **(1.5-qt./1.5-L) Saucepan**; heat over medium heat 1-3 minutes or until shimmering. Add rice; stir until well coated with oil. Add broth; bring to a boil. Cover; reduce heat to low and simmer 5 minutes. Remove from heat.

2. Meanwhile, for chicken, add oil to **(10-in./25-cm) Sauté Pan**; heat over medium-high heat 1-3 minutes or until shimmering. Season chicken with salt and black pepper. Cook chicken 3-5 minutes or until golden brown. Turn chicken over; cook 3-5 minutes or until center of chicken is no longer pink. Remove chicken from pan to a plate; tent with aluminum foil.

3. For sauce, reduce heat to medium; add tomato paste to same Sauté Pan and cook over medium heat 2 minutes or until tomato paste is caramelized, whisking constantly with **Silicone Flat Whisk**. Add water and pressed garlic; simmer 2-3 minutes or until sauce begins to thicken, whisking to loosen browned bits from bottom of pan.

4. As sauce simmers, cut olives lengthwise into quarters. Peel tomatoes using **Serrated Peeler**. Remove cores and seeds using **Core & More**. Slice tomatoes lengthwise into thin strips. Add chicken, olives and tomatoes to sauce; simmer until heated through.

5. To serve, divide rice between serving plates; top with chicken.

Yield: 2 servings

U.S. Nutrients per serving: Calories 440, Total Fat 16 g, Saturated Fat 2 g, Cholesterol 65 mg, Carbohydrate 41 g, Protein 32 g, Sodium 1430 mg, Fiber 4 g

U.S. Diabetic exchanges per serving: 3 starch, 3 low-fat meat, 1 fat (3 carb)

CHEF'S CORNER

The Serrated Peeler eliminates the blanching step in peeling tomatoes. The Core & More completely cleans out the inside of the tomato so that the sauce won't become watered down. Cutting the tomato into thin strips gives this dish a rustic but elegant presentation.

Combining instant rice with oil or butter results in better flavor and a firmer texture.

25 minutes

CURRIED CHICKEN WITH COUSCOUS

Coconut milk and curry powder are the keys to this recipe's authenticity, and they are both easily found in most supermarkets.

CHICKEN AND CURRY

- 1 lb (500 g) boneless, skinless chicken breasts
- ¾ tsp (4 mL) salt
- ¼ tsp (1 mL) coarsely ground black pepper
- 4 medium carrots
- 1 medium onion
- 1 tsp (5 mL) vegetable oil
- 2 tsp (10 mL) curry powder

- ½ cup (125 mL) golden raisins
- 1 can (13.5 oz/398 mL) coconut milk

COUSCOUS

- 2 cups (500 mL) chicken broth
- 1⅓ cups (325 mL) uncooked plain couscous
- 1 tbsp (15 mL) butter
- 2 tbsp (30 mL) snipped fresh cilantro plus additional for garnish

1. For chicken, cut chicken into 1-in. (2.5-cm) pieces. Lightly spray **(10-in./25-cm) Skillet** with vegetable oil using **Kitchen Spritzer**. Heat Skillet over medium-high heat 1-3 minutes or until hot. As Skillet heats, combine salt and black pepper in **Prep Bowl**. Season chicken with half of the black pepper mixture. Cook chicken about 2-3 minutes or until golden brown. Turn chicken over; cook 2-3 minutes or until center of chicken is no longer pink. Remove from Skillet; set aside.

2. As chicken cooks, peel carrots; cut in half lengthwise, then thinly slice on a bias. Cut onion in half lengthwise, then crosswise into ½-in. (1-cm) wedges. Add oil to Skillet. Sauté carrots and onion 5 minutes or until crisp-tender, stirring occasionally. Stir curry powder, raisins, coconut milk and remaining black pepper mixture into Skillet. Add chicken; simmer 3-5 minutes or until sauce begins to thicken.

3. Meanwhile, for couscous, pour broth into **Rice Cooker Plus**; cover and microwave on HIGH 3 minutes or until boiling. Stir couscous and butter into broth. Cover; let stand 5 minutes. As couscous stands, snip cilantro using **Kitchen Shears**. Fluff couscous with a fork; stir in cilantro.

4. To serve, divide couscous among serving plates; spoon chicken mixture over couscous. Garnish with additional snipped cilantro.

Yield: 4 servings

U.S. Nutrients per serving: Calories 660, Total Fat 23 g, Saturated Fat 14 g, Cholesterol 75 mg, Carbohydrate 72 g, Protein 38 g, Sodium 850 mg, Fiber 6 g

U.S. Diabetic exchanges per serving: 5 starch, 3 low-fat meat, 2 fat (5 carb)

CHEF'S CORNER

Coconut milk is made by mixing the grated meat of a ripe coconut with warm water and then squeezing out the juice. Coconut milk is sold in cans. Always shake or stir the coconut milk before using. "Lite" coconut milk, made from the second squeezing of the coconut meat and water, is less creamy and flavorful than regular coconut milk.

Couscous, a coarsely ground semolina pasta, is a staple in many North African countries. Couscous is sold pre-cooked in the United States, making it a quick side dish. You can find couscous in the rice or pasta section of most grocery stores.

29 minutes

npp

This restaurant-style dish combines artichokes, Parmesan cheese and rosemary for an authentic Italian flavor.

POTATOES AND CHICKEN

- 3 small red potatoes
- 1½ cups (375 mL) water
- 1 tsp (5 mL) salt
- 2 boneless, skinless chicken breasts (4-6 oz/125-175 g each)
- 2 tsp (10 mL) **Rosemary Herb Seasoning Mix**, divided
- 2 tsp (10 mL) olive oil, divided

ARTICHOKE TOPPING

- ½ cup (125 mL) chopped artichoke hearts (about 2 hearts)
- 2 tsp (10 mL) chopped fresh parsley
- 1 oz (30 g) Parmesan cheese, divided
- 2 tsp (10 mL) mayonnaise

1. Preheat broiler on HIGH. Meanwhile, cut potatoes into quarters. Place potatoes, water and salt into **Small Micro-Cooker®**; microwave on HIGH 6-8 minutes or until tender. Drain and set aside.

2. Meanwhile, for artichoke topping, chop artichokes and parsley using **Santoku Knife**; place into **Small Batter Bowl**. Grate cheese using **Microplane® Adjustable Grater**. Set aside 2 tbsp (30 mL) for later use; add remaining cheese and mayonnaise to artichoke mixture and mix well.

3. Flatten chicken to ½ in. (1 cm) thickness using flat side of **Meat Tenderizer**. Sprinkle both sides of chicken with 1 tsp (5 mL) of the seasoning mix.

4. Add 1 tsp (5 mL) of the oil to **Stainless (10-in./25-cm) Skillet** (do not use nonstick cookware); heat over medium-high heat 1-3 minutes or until shimmering. Meanwhile, add remaining 1 tsp (5 mL) of the oil and remaining 1 tsp (5 mL) of the seasoning mix to potatoes; stir to coat.

5. Place chicken and potatoes, cut side down, into Skillet. Cook 3-4 minutes or until chicken is golden brown. Turn chicken and potatoes over; cook an additional 3-4 minutes or until chicken is golden brown and centers are no longer pink.

6. Remove potatoes from Skillet; set aside and keep warm. To finish chicken, spread artichoke topping evenly over chicken; sprinkle with reserved cheese. Place Skillet as close as possible to heating element (2 in./5 cm); broil 4-6 minutes or until topping is deep golden brown and internal temperature of chicken registers 170°F (77°C). (Watch closely. If topping starts to brown unevenly, adjust accordingly.) Carefully remove Skillet from broiler. Serve chicken with potatoes.

Yield: 2 servings

U.S. Nutrients per serving: Calories 320, Total Fat 14 g, Saturated Fat 4 g, Cholesterol 80 mg, Carbohydrate 21 g, Protein 34 g, Sodium 1280 mg, Fiber 3 g

U.S. Diabetic exchanges per serving: 1½ starch, 4 low-fat meat, 1 fat (1½ carb)

CHEF'S CORNER

Stainless cookware is excellent for its ability to withstand high heat. Topping each chicken breast with Parmesan cheese and placing them under the broiler results in a delicious and attractive-looking crust.

Placing the potatoes cut side down in the Skillet allows them to brown. When turning over the chicken breasts, turn the potatoes to their other cut side using **Chef's Tongs** to ensure even browning.

1 tsp (5 mL) crushed dried rosemary leaves, ¼ tsp (1 mL) salt and ⅛ tsp (0.5 mL) coarsely ground black pepper can be substituted for the Rosemary Herb Seasoning Mix, if desired.

28 minutes

PAPRIKA CHICKEN & EGG NOODLES

Cooking noodles and green beans in the same pot, then using some of the pasta cooking water for the pan sauce, creates an efficient version of a classic Hungarian dish.

8 oz (250 g) green beans	8 oz (250 g) mushrooms
1 lb (500 g) boneless, skinless chicken thighs	1 medium onion
1 tbsp (15 mL) paprika	3 tbsp (45 mL) butter, divided
½ tsp (2 mL) salt	8 oz (250 g) uncooked egg noodles
¼ tsp (1 mL) coarsely ground black pepper	2 tbsp (30 mL) snipped fresh dill
¼ tsp (1 mL) cayenne pepper (optional)	Sour cream (optional)

1. For noodles, bring salted water to a boil in **(4-qt./4-L) Casserole**. Cut green beans diagonally into 2-in. (5-cm) pieces. Set aside.

2. Lightly spray **(12-in./30-cm) Skillet** with vegetable oil using **Kitchen Spritzer**; heat over medium-high heat 1-3 minutes or until hot. Meanwhile, dice chicken into 1-in. (2.5-cm) pieces; sprinkle with paprika, salt, black pepper and cayenne pepper, if desired. Cook 5-7 minutes or until centers of chicken are no longer pink, stirring occasionally. Remove chicken from Skillet; set aside.

3. As chicken cooks, cut mushrooms into quarters. Cut onion in half lengthwise; then into ½-in. (1-cm) wedges. Add 1 tbsp (15 mL) of the butter to Skillet. Cook and stir mushrooms and onion over medium-high heat 5 minutes or until golden brown.

4. Meanwhile, add noodles to Casserole and cook 2 minutes. Add green beans to noodles. Cook, uncovered, 5-6 minutes or until noodles are cooked to desired tenderness. Carefully remove ¾ cup (75 mL) of the cooking water for use in sauce. Drain noodles and green beans using large **Colander**.

5. Add chicken and cooking water to Skillet; stir to loosen browned bits from bottom of Skillet using **Silicone Flat Whisk**. Cook and stir 2-3 minutes or until sauce is thickened and chicken is heated through.

6. Meanwhile, toss noodles and green beans with remaining 2 tbsp (30 mL) butter. Snip dill using **Kitchen Shears**. To serve, divide noodle mixture among serving plates; top with chicken. Sprinkle with dill and garnish with sour cream, if desired.

Yield: 4 servings

U.S. Nutrients per serving: Calories 500, Total Fat 20 g, Saturated Fat 8 g, Cholesterol 150 mg, Carbohydrate 49 g, Protein 31 g, Sodium 380 mg, Fiber 5 g

U.S. Diabetic exchanges per serving: 3 starch, 3 medium-fat meat (3 carb)

CHEF'S CORNER

Paprika is made by grinding dried, aromatic sweet red peppers, most of which come from Spain, South America, California and Hungary. The flavor of paprika can vary from sweet to smoky to spicy. However, paprika only releases its full color and flavor when it is heated. Paprika loses its flavor quickly, so it should be purchased in small quantities and stored in a cool, dark place for no more than 6 months.

This dish is also called chicken paprikash, a Hungarian dish with chicken, onions and paprika. It is typically served with sour cream.

29 minutes

TURKEY GYROS

In just 28 minutes, you can create a light version of gyros that rivals the real thing, thanks to a blend of herbs and a special mixing technique.

GYROS

- ½ small onion
- 2 tbsp (30 mL) chopped fresh Italian parsley
- 2 garlic cloves, pressed
- 1 lb (500 g) 93% lean ground turkey
- ½ tsp (2 mL) dried thyme
- ½ tsp (2 mL) salt
- ½ tsp (2 mL) coarsely ground black pepper
- 2 tsp (10 mL) olive oil

- 4 flat pita bread rounds (without pockets)
- Sliced cucumber and sliced tomatoes

YOGURT SAUCE

- ½ cup (125 mL) plain yogurt
- 2 garlic cloves, pressed
- ⅛ tsp (0.5 mL) salt
- 2 tbsp (30 mL) chopped fresh Italian parsley
- ¼ cup (50 mL) fresh cucumber, finely chopped

CHEF'S CORNER

The Bread Knife's serrated edge gives you the control of cutting the loaves into thin slices. Use gentle pressure when cutting with the Bread Knife; the blade should do most of the work.

The authentic look and texture of these gyros is achieved by vigorously mixing the meat with the **Mix 'N Scraper®** and thinly slicing the turkey loaves. The vigorous mixing helps bind the proteins in the turkey, making it easier to slice after cooking.

If desired, this recipe can be prepared in a nonstick skillet if a lower temperature is used. Preheat oven to 350°F (180°C). Proceed as recipe directs, omitting oil and baking 11-13 minutes.

1. To start gyros, preheat oven to 500°F (260°C). Finely chop onion using **Food Chopper**. Chop all parsley with **Santoku Knife**; set aside 2 tbsp (30 mL) of the parsley for sauce. Press garlic into **Stainless (4-qt./4-L) Mixing Bowl**; add onion, 2 tbsp (30 mL) of the parsley, turkey, thyme, ½ tsp (2 mL) of the salt and black pepper. Mix vigorously until well blended.

2. Add oil to **Stainless (10-in./25-cm) Skillet** (see Chef's Corner for nonstick cookware instructions); heat over medium-high heat 1-3 minutes or until shimmering. As oil heats, form turkey mixture into four thin, rectangular loaves, about ¼ in. (6 mm) thick. Cook 1-2 minutes on each side or until browned. Place Skillet in oven and bake 6-8 minutes or until internal temperature reaches 165°F (74°C) and loaves are no longer pink in center.

3. Meanwhile, prepare sauce. In **Small Batter Bowl**, combine yogurt, pressed garlic, salt and reserved parsley. Chop cucumber using Food Chopper; add to batter bowl and mix well.

4. To finish gyros, place pita bread into **Deep Dish Baker** and microwave on HIGH 30-60 seconds; transfer to serving plates. Meanwhile, slice cucumbers and tomatoes.

5. Remove turkey loaves from oven. Thinly slice lengthwise using **Bread Knife**; arrange over pita bread. To serve, top each gyro with 1 tbsp (15 mL) yogurt sauce; serve with sliced cucumber and sliced tomatoes, if desired.

Yield: 4 servings

Light • U.S. Nutrients per serving: Calories 410, Total Fat 14 g, Saturated Fat 3.5 g, Cholesterol 70 mg, Carbohydrate 41 g, Protein 32 g, Sodium 810 mg, Fiber 4 g

U.S. Diabetic exchanges per serving: 2 starch, 2 vegetable, 3 low-fat meat (2 carb)

28 minutes

SKILLET LASAGNA

This family favorite delivers all of the flavor of lasagna in half of the time. Spicy turkey sausage boosts the flavor.

1 jar (24-26 oz or 680-700 mL) marinara sauce

3 cups (750 mL) water

8 oz (250 g) lasagna noodles

1 lb (500 g) bulk hot Italian turkey sausage or sausage links, casings removed

2 garlic cloves, pressed

2 oz (60 g) Parmesan cheese

2 tbsp (30 mL) chopped fresh parsley, divided

1 cup (250 mL) fresh whole milk ricotta cheese (about 8 oz/250 g, see Chef's Corner)

½ cup (125 mL) shredded mozzarella cheese

¼ tsp (1 mL) coarsely ground black pepper

Additional grated Parmesan cheese (optional)

1. Combine sauce and water in **(12-in./30-cm) Skillet**. Cover; bring to a boil.

2. Meanwhile, wrap noodles in clean kitchen towel and break crosswise into quarters. Stir noodles into sauce. Cover; reduce heat and simmer 16-18 minutes or until noodles are tender, stirring occasionally.

3. As noodles cook, place sausage into **(10-in./25-cm) Skillet**; cook and stir over medium-high heat 6-8 minutes or until sausage is no longer pink, breaking into crumbles using **Mix 'N Chop**. Add pressed garlic; cook 1 minute. Remove from heat. Stir sausage into noodles and sauce.

4. Meanwhile, grate Parmesan cheese using **Deluxe Cheese Grater**. Chop parsley using **Santoku Knife**; set aside 1 tbsp (15 mL) parsley for garnish. Combine cheeses, remaining parsley and black pepper in **Classic Batter Bowl**. Scoop cheese mixture over noodles using **Medium Scoop**. Cover Skillet and simmer gently 3-5 minutes or until cheese is melted and ricotta mixture is heated through.

5. To serve, sprinkle lasagna with reserved parsley and additional Parmesan cheese, if desired.

Yield: 6 servings

U.S. Nutrients per serving: Calories 470, Total Fat 21 g, Saturated Fat 9 g, Cholesterol 80 mg, Carbohydrate 41 g, Protein 30 g, Sodium 1200 mg, Fiber 3 g

U.S. Diabetic exchanges per serving: 3 starch, 3 medium-fat meat (3 carb)

CHEF'S CORNER

Wrapping lasagna noodles in a clean kitchen towel before breaking into quarters prevents them from scattering around your countertop.

The attractive ruffled edge of regular lasagna noodles adds to this dish's visual appeal. No-boil noodles can be used instead of the regular lasagna noodles, if desired. Reduce cooking time of noodles to 10-12 minutes; proceed as recipe directs.

Fresh whole milk ricotta cheese is preferred in this recipe for its smooth texture. Look for fresh ricotta cheese at the deli. Drain off excess liquid before using.

29 minutes

PECAN-CRUSTED CHICKEN WITH SWEET MUSTARD DRESSING

The pecan crust develops a pleasing crunch when you pan-fry the chicken strips.

CHICKEN

- 1 egg white
- 1½ cups (375 mL) pecans
- ½ tsp (2 mL) salt
- ¼ tsp (1 mL) cayenne pepper
- 6 chicken tenders (about 1 lb/500 g)
- ¼ cup (50 mL) vegetable oil

DRESSING AND GREENS

- ¼ cup (50 mL) peach preserves
- 2 tbsp (30 mL) prepared stone-ground mustard
- 1 tsp (5 mL) cider vinegar
- ¼ tsp (1 mL) salt
- ¼ tsp (1 mL) coarsely ground black pepper
- 1 garlic clove, pressed
- 2 tbsp (30 mL) vegetable oil
- 4 cups (1 L) mixed baby greens

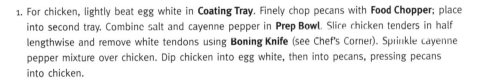

1. For chicken, lightly beat egg white in **Coating Tray**. Finely chop pecans with **Food Chopper**; place into second tray. Combine salt and cayenne pepper in **Prep Bowl**. Slice chicken tenders in half lengthwise and remove white tendons using **Boning Knife** (see Chef's Corner). Sprinkle cayenne pepper mixture over chicken. Dip chicken into egg white, then into pecans, pressing pecans into chicken.

2. Add oil to **(12-in./30-cm) Skillet**; heat over medium-low heat 1-3 minutes or until shimmering. Cook chicken 2-3 minutes or until deep golden brown. Turn chicken over; cook an additional 2-3 minutes or until centers of chicken are no longer pink.

3. Meanwhile, for dressing, whisk together preserves, mustard, vinegar, salt, black pepper, pressed garlic and oil in **Small Batter Bowl**.

4. To serve, toss greens with 2 tbsp (30 mL) of the dressing; divide among serving plates. Drizzle remaining dressing around edge of plates. Arrange three of the chicken strips around each salad.

Yield: 4 servings

U.S. Nutrients per serving: Calories 580, Total Fat 43 g, Saturated Fat 4 g, Cholesterol 65 mg, Carbohydrate 23 g, Protein 32 g, Sodium 620 mg, Fiber 6 g

U.S. Diabetic exchanges per serving: 1 fruit, 4½ low-fat meat, 6 fat (1 carb)

CHEF'S CORNER

Chicken tenders have a thin white tendon that can be eaten, but is often tough and stringy when cooked. To remove tendons for this recipe, slice alongside one side of the tendon while cutting the tender in half lengthwise. Then, carefully trim tendon.

If desired, four chicken breast halves (4-6 oz/125-175 g each), cut into three strips for a total of 12 strips, can be substituted for the chicken tenders.

Make sure the heat for cooking the chicken is not too high, or the pecan coating will burn before the chicken is cooked through.

29 minutes

TURKEY SALTIMBOCCA

Thin turkey cutlets are the key to quick cooking in this Italian-inspired dish, flavored with prosciutto and fresh sage.

2 tbsp (30 mL) thinly sliced fresh sage

1 oz (30 g) Parmesan cheese

3 tbsp (45 mL) all-purpose flour

3 tsp (15 mL) olive oil, divided

8 turkey breast cutlets (about 1 lb/500 g)

8 thin slices prosciutto (about 4 oz/125 g)

½ cup (125 mL) reduced-sodium chicken broth

3 tbsp (45 mL) butter

1. Thinly slice sage using **Santoku Knife** and set aside. Grate cheese into **Coating Tray** using **Microplane® Adjustable Grater** and toss with flour. Add 2 tsp (10 mL) of the oil to **(12-in./30-cm) Skillet**; heat over medium-high heat 1-3 minutes or until shimmering.

2. As Skillet heats, place one cutlet into cheese mixture; sprinkle with sage. Place one slice of prosciutto over sage, trimming or folding to fit. Press to adhere. Turn cutlet to coat and lay in second tray. Repeat with remaining cutlets.

3. Place half of the coated cutlets into Skillet, prosciutto side down, and cook 3-4 minutes or until golden brown. Turn cutlets using **Small Slotted Turner**; cook an additional 30 seconds and transfer to serving platter. Place remaining 1 tsp (5 mL) oil in Skillet; cook remaining cutlets and transfer to serving platter.

4. Immediately add broth and butter to same Skillet using **Silicone Flat Whisk**, stirring to loosen browned bits. Continue whisking until butter is melted and sauce comes to a boil.

5. To serve, pour sauce over cutlets and serve immediately.

Yield: 4 servings

U.S. Nutrients per serving: Calories 340, Total Fat 18 g, Saturated Fat 9 g, Cholesterol 100 mg, Carbohydrate 6 g, Protein 40 g, Sodium 910 mg, Fiber 0 g

U.S. Diabetic exchanges per serving: ½ starch, 4 medium-fat meat (½ carb)

CHEF'S CORNER

Use Coating Trays to coat both sides of the turkey cutlets. The side-by-side trays allow you to coat the cutlets in one tray and move them to another tray in an assembly-line fashion with little mess.

Prosciutto is Italian-style ham that has been seasoned, salt-cured and air-dried but not smoked. Prosciutto has a salty, yet sweet, flavor with a smooth texture. Domestic prosciutto is less expensive than imported prosciutto. For this recipe, look for very thinly sliced prosciutto.

Chicken breasts or pork tenderloin medallions, pounded thinly, can be substituted for the turkey breast cutlets, if desired.

25 minutes

CRUNCHY WHOLE-GRAIN CHICKEN BITES

These family-friendly chicken bites can be made Buffalo style with the addition of hot sauce and blue cheese.

DRESSING AND SLAW

- ½ cup (125 mL) reduced-fat sour cream
- 2 tbsp (30 mL) reduced-fat mayonnaise
- 1 pkg (1 oz/28 g) dry ranch dressing mix, divided
- 5 stalks celery
- 2 carrots

CHICKEN BITES

- 1 lb (500 g) chicken tenders
- Remaining dry ranch dressing mix from dressing, divided
- 1 egg white
- 6 cups (1.5 L) whole-grain chips (5 oz/150 g)
- ¼ tsp (1 mL) paprika
- Vegetable oil
- Hot sauce and crumbled blue cheese (optional)

CHEF'S CORNER

Whole-grain chips and ranch dressing mix give these chicken bites a unique flavor. The crunchy coating helps keep the tenders moist, and baking on the stone keeps the coating crisp.

Slicing celery thinly on a bias creates an interesting slaw. Keep the slaw crisp by combining with the dressing just before serving.

Avoid cross-contamination by using separate cutting boards and knives to prepare the chicken and slaw.

1. Preheat oven to 400°F (200°C). For dressing, in **Small Batter Bowl**, whisk together sour cream, mayonnaise and 1 tbsp (15 mL) of the dressing mix (reserve remaining dressing mix for chicken); set aside.

2. For chicken, cut chicken tenders into 1½-in. (4-cm) pieces. Whisk together 1 tbsp (15 mL) of the reserved dressing mix and egg white in **Classic Batter Bowl**. Crush chips using flat side of **Meat Tenderizer** in resealable plastic bag; add remaining dressing mix and paprika and shake well.

3. Add chicken to egg white mixture; mix well to coat. Add half of the coated chicken to crumb mixture; shake to coat with crumbs and arrange in a single layer on **Rectangle Stone**. Repeat with remaining coated chicken and crumbs.

4. Spray chicken generously with oil using **Kitchen Spritzer**. Bake 14-16 minutes or until chicken is golden brown and centers are no longer pink. Remove from oven.

5. Meanwhile, for slaw, thinly slice celery on the bias. Peel carrots; cut into julienne strips using **Julienne Peeler**. Combine celery and carrots with ¼ cup (50 mL) of the dressing; mix well. To serve, divide chicken and slaw among serving plates; serve with remaining dressing for dipping. If desired, drizzle chicken with hot sauce and crumble blue cheese over dressing.

Yield: 4 servings

U.S. Nutrients per serving: Calories 390, Total Fat 13 g, Saturated Fat 4 g, Cholesterol 80 mg, Carbohydrate 36 g, Protein 31 g, Sodium 880 mg, Fiber 5 g

U.S. Diabetic exchanges per serving: 2 starch, 3½ low-fat meat, ½ fat (2 carb)

29 minutes

GLAZED CHICKEN WITH APPLE SALAD

Apples and watercress create a lively twist on cole slaw. Pounding chicken breasts to an even thickness allows them to cook in less than 12 minutes.

DRESSING AND APPLE SALAD

- 2 tbsp (30 mL) cider vinegar
- 2 tbsp (30 mL) apple jelly
- 1/3 cup (75 mL) reduced-fat mayonnaise
- 1 Granny Smith apple
- 1 red apple such as Jonathan, McIntosh or Gala
- 1/2 cup (125 mL) lightly packed watercress plus additional for serving

CHICKEN AND GLAZE

- 4 boneless, skinless chicken breasts (4-6 oz/125-175 g each)
- 1 tbsp (15 mL) olive oil
- 1/2 tsp (1 mL) salt
- 1/4 tsp (1 mL) coarsely ground black pepper
- 2 tbsp (30 mL) apple jelly
- 1 tsp (5 mL) prepared stone-ground mustard
- 1 tbsp (15 mL) brown sugar

CHEF'S CORNER

To julienne an apple, cut apple into quarters; set cut side down and cut out core at an angle. Thinly slice apple lengthwise; cut slices into thin strips.

Apricot jam can be substituted for the apple jelly, if desired.

Dijon mustard can be substituted for the stone-ground mustard.

Watercress is a member of the mustard family. It is available in small bunches all year long. When buying watercress, look for crisp green leaves.

To wash watercress, fill the spinner bowl of **Salad & Berry Spinner** with cold water. Fill the colander with watercress, dunk it in the water and swish to release dirt. Spin dry.

1. For dressing, mix together vinegar, jelly and mayonnaise in **Measure, Mix & Pour™**; set aside. For salad, slice apples into julienne strips (see Chef's Corner). Remove leaves from watercress stems (discard stems); coarsely chop watercress leaves. Combine apples and watercress in **Classic Batter Bowl**; set aside.

2. For chicken, heat **Grill Pan** over medium-high heat 5 minutes. Meanwhile, flatten chicken to an even thickness using **Meat Tenderizer**. Brush with oil and season with salt and black pepper. Cook chicken 4-6 minutes or until grill marks appear. Turn chicken over; cook 4-6 minutes or until center of chicken is no longer pink.

3. While chicken is cooking, prepare glaze. Combine jelly, mustard and brown sugar in **Prep Bowl**. Brush chicken with glaze during last minute of cooking.

4. To serve, arrange additional watercress on serving plates, if desired. Pour dressing over salad just before serving; toss gently to coat. Top watercress with salad and chicken.

Yield: 4 servings

U.S. Nutrients per serving: Calories 280, Total Fat 7 g, Saturated Fat 1.5 g, Cholesterol 65 mg, Carbohydrate 28 g, Protein 26 g, Sodium 560 mg, Fiber 1 g

U.S. Diabetic exchanges per serving: 2 fruit, 4 low-fat meat (2 carb)

26 minutes

TEX-MEX CHICKEN & RICE SKILLET

This one-skillet meal is packed with flavor due to the purchased salsa verde that delivers zip while allowing you to choose your own heat level.

- 1 tsp plus 1 tbsp (5 mL plus 15 mL) vegetable oil, divided
- 1 can (11 oz or 341 mL) Mexican-style corn
- 1 lb (500 mL) boneless, skinless chicken thighs
- 1 tbsp (15 mL) **Southwestern Seasoning Mix**
- 2 cups (500 mL) uncooked instant white rice
- 2 cups (500 mL) chicken broth
- 1½ cups (375 mL) salsa verde
- 2 tbsp (30 mL) snipped fresh cilantro
- 1 cup (250 mL) shredded Mexican cheese blend

1. Add 1 tsp (5 mL) of the oil to **(12-in./30-cm) Skillet**; heat over medium-high heat 1-3 minutes or until shimmering. Meanwhile, drain corn; pat dry with paper towels. Add corn to Skillet in a single layer. Cook without stirring 5 minutes or until caramelized on one side. Remove corn from Skillet; set aside.

2. As corn cooks, cut chicken into 1-in. (2.5-cm) pieces using **Chef's Knife**. Combine chicken and seasoning mix in **Classic Batter Bowl**. Add chicken to Skillet. Cook over medium-high heat 5-7 minutes or until center of chicken is no longer pink, stirring occasionally. Remove chicken from Skillet; set aside.

3. Add remaining 1 tbsp (15 mL) oil to Skillet. Add rice; stir until well coated with oil. Add broth and salsa; bring to a simmer over medium-high heat. Cover Skillet; reduce heat to low. Simmer 5 minutes or until most of the liquid is absorbed. Meanwhile, snip cilantro using **Kitchen Shears**.

4. To serve, spoon chicken over rice mixture in Skillet. Sprinkle with cheese and corn. Cover; let stand 5 minutes or until cheese is melted. Sprinkle with cilantro.

Yield: 6 servings

Light • U.S. Nutrients per serving: Calories 570, Total Fat 12 g, Saturated Fat 5g, Cholesterol 80 mg, Carbohydrate 83 g, Protein 26 g, Sodium 860 mg, Fiber 1 g

U.S. Diabetic exchanges per serving: 5½ starch, 1 medium-fat meat, 1 fat (5½ carb)

CHEF'S CORNER

Caramelizing the corn intensifies the sweetness and adds an interesting color and texture.

Combining instant rice with oil or butter results in better flavor and a firmer texture.

Taco seasoning mix can be substituted for the Southwestern Seasoning Mix, if desired.

28 minutes

ALMOND CHICKEN STIR-FRY

This flavorful stir-fry tastes even more authentic when served over a pan-fried noodle cake.

CHICKEN

- 1 egg white
- 1 tbsp (15 mL) cornstarch
- 1 seasoning packet from 1 pkg (3 oz or 85 g) chicken-flavored ramen noodles
- 1 lb (500 g) chicken tenders
- 1 tbsp (15 mL) vegetable oil

STIR-FRY

- 1 tbsp (15 mL) grated fresh gingerroot
- 2 garlic cloves, pressed
- ¼ cup (50 mL) slivered almonds, divided

- 1 tbsp (15 mL) cornstarch
- 1½ cups (375 mL) chicken broth
- 8 oz (250 g) snow peas
- 1 can (about 15 oz or 398 g) baby corn, drained
- 1 can (8 oz or 199 mL) water chestnuts, drained
- ½ tsp (2 mL) coarsely ground black pepper

Pan-Fried Noodle Cake (see Chef's Corner)

1. For chicken, lightly whisk egg white in **Classic Batter Bowl**. Add cornstarch and seasoning packet; whisk well. Slice chicken tenders on the bias into ½-in. (1-cm) pieces. Toss chicken with egg white mixture; set aside.

2. For stir-fry, grate gingerroot into **Prep Bowl** using **Microplane® Adjustable Grater**; add pressed garlic and set aside. Place almonds into **Stir-Fry Skillet**; cook and stir over medium-high heat 3-4 minutes or until toasted. Remove almonds from Skillet and set aside.

3. Prepare *Pan-Fried Noodle Cake* (see Chef's Corner). As noodle cake cooks, stir-fry chicken. Add oil to same Stir-Fry Skillet; heat over medium-high heat 1-3 minutes or until shimmering. Add coated chicken pieces to Skillet. Cook and stir 4-6 minutes or until centers of chicken are no longer pink. Remove from Skillet and keep warm.

4. To finish stir-fry, whisk together cornstarch and broth in **Small Batter Bowl**; add to Skillet. Bring to a simmer, stirring frequently. Add gingerroot and garlic to Skillet; heat until fragrant, stirring constantly. Add vegetables and chicken to Skillet; simmer 1-2 minutes or until heated through. Stir in half of the toasted almonds. Serve stir-fry over noodle cake; sprinkle with remaining almonds and black pepper.

Yield: 4 servings

Light • U.S. Nutrients per serving (including noodle cake): Calories 540, Total Fat 17 g, Saturated Fat 4.5 g, Cholesterol 65 mg, Carbohydrate 63 g, Protein 39 g, Sodium 1190 mg, Fiber 8 g

U.S. Diabetic exchanges per serving (including noodle cake): 4 starch, 3 medium-fat meat (4 carb)

CHEF'S CORNER

Pan-Fried Noodle Cake: Place 2 cups (500 mL) water into **Large Micro-Cooker®**. Microwave on HIGH 2-3 minutes or until boiling; add 2 pkg (3 oz or 85 g each) chicken-flavored ramen noodles. Microwave on HIGH 3 minutes or until softened; drain. Lightly spray (**10-in./ 25-cm) Sauté Pan** with vegetable oil; heat over medium-high heat 1-3 minutes or until hot. Combine noodles with 1 tbsp (15 mL) oil and 1 seasoning packet from ramen noodles. Add noodles to pan; gently press to form a cake. Cook 3-4 minutes on each side or until golden brown. Cut into wedges.

Slicing chicken tenders on a bias and coating them with egg white and cornstarch gives them a tender, velvety texture.

28 minutes

BERRY-PINE NUT CHICKEN SALAD

Using cooked chicken and bagged lettuce shaves off a great deal of time for this summertime salad.

DRESSING

- 3 tbsp (45 mL) red wine vinegar
- 2 tbsp (30 mL) seedless raspberry jam
- 1 tsp (5 mL) Dijon mustard
- ¼ cup (50 mL) olive oil
- ⅛ tsp (0.5 mL) salt
- ⅛ tsp (0.5 mL) coarsely ground black pepper

SALAD

- ¼ cup (50 mL) pine nuts
- 1 bag (5-6 oz/150-175 g) Boston lettuce salad blend (about 5 cups/125 L torn Boston lettuce)
- 1 cup (250 mL) blueberries
- 1 lb (500 g) cooked chicken breasts (about 4)
- ¼ small red onion
- 8 oz (250 g) sugar snap peas (2 cups/500 mL)

1. For dressing, combine vinegar, jam and mustard in **Measure, Mix & Pour™**; mix well. Add oil, salt and black pepper. Mix again and set aside.

2. For salad, place pine nuts into **(8-in./20-cm) Sauté Pan**; toast over medium heat 4-6 minutes or until fragrant and golden brown. Remove pine nuts from pan; cool completely.

3. Wash lettuce and berries using **Salad & Berry Spinner**. Thinly slice chicken and onion using **Chef's Knife**. Cut sugar snap peas in half on a bias.

4. To serve, layer lettuce, chicken, peas, blueberries and onion in a large serving bowl. Pour dressing over salad just before serving; toss gently to coat. Sprinkle with toasted pine nuts.

Yield: 4 servings

U.S. Nutrients per serving: Calories 450, Total Fat 24 g, Saturated Fat 3.5 g, Cholesterol 95 mg, Carbohydrate 20 g, Protein 39 g, Sodium 200 mg, Fiber 3 g

U.S. Diabetic exchanges per serving: 1 fruit, 1 vegetable, 4 low-fat meat, 3 fat (1 carb)

CHEF'S CORNER

Using seedless raspberry jam in the vinaigrette adds concentrated raspberry flavor. If desired, use raspberry vinegar in place of the red wine vinegar for even greater impact.

Pine nuts can be toasted in the **Small Oval Baker** in the microwave oven for 2-3 minutes, stirring after each 30-second interval.

This salad can be served in the outer bowl of the Salad & Berry Spinner for casual meals.

15 minutes

CHICKEN POSOLE VERDE

Pronounced (po-SO-lay), rotisserie or leftover chicken makes this home-style Mexican stew ready to serve in just 20 minutes.

- 1 tbsp (15 mL) olive oil
- 2 garlic cloves, pressed
- 1 can (29 oz/857 mL) white hominy, drained
- 2 cups (500 mL) chicken broth
- 1 can (10 oz/295 mL) medium green enchilada sauce
- 1 cup (250 mL) water

- 1 tsp (5 mL) dried Mexican oregano
- 2 cups (500 mL) diced cooked chicken (12 oz/350 g)
- 1 cup (250 mL) thinly sliced green cabbage
- 2 tbsp (30 mL) chopped fresh cilantro
- 1 lime

1. Add oil and pressed garlic to **(4-qt./4-L) Casserole**; heat over medium-high heat 1-3 minutes or until garlic is golden brown and fragrant. Meanwhile, drain hominy using large **Colander**.

2. Immediately add broth, enchilada sauce, water, oregano and hominy to Casserole; bring to boil. Reduce heat to medium; simmer 8 minutes.

3. As hominy mixture comes to a boil, dice chicken using **Santoku Knife**. Add chicken to Casserole; simmer until heated through.

4. As posole simmers, thinly slice cabbage and chop cilantro. Slice lime into wedges.

5. To serve, divide posole among serving bowls; top with cabbage. Garnish with cilantro and lime wedges.

Yield: 4 servings

U.S. Nutrients per serving: Calories 290, Total Fat 11 g, Saturated Fat 2 g, Cholesterol 60 mg, Carbohydrate 22 g, Protein 23 g, Sodium 830 mg, Fiber 5 g

U.S. Diabetic exchanges per serving: 1 starch, 3 medium-fat meat (1 carb)

CHEF'S CORNER

Hominy is made from large, starchy dried white or yellow corn kernels from which the hull and germ have been removed. The corn is then rehydrated, which gives it a distinct flavor and texture.

Mexican oregano has a stronger flavor than its Mediterranean counterpart and can be found in Hispanic markets or in the gourmet spice section of larger supermarkets. If Mexican oregano cannot be found, Mediterranean oregano can be substituted.

Green salsa or salsa verde can be substituted for the enchilada sauce, if desired.

20 minutes

MEDITERRANEAN QUESADILLAS WITH ANTIPASTO RELISH

This play on quesadillas starts off with cooked chicken, a great use for "planned-overs." All four quesadillas fit on the griddle at the same time for quick cooking.

ANTIPASTO RELISH

- ½ cup (125 mL) jarred roasted red peppers, drained
- ¼ cup (50 mL) pitted kalamata olives
- ¼ cup (50 mL) pepperoncini
- 1 tbsp (15 mL) chopped fresh basil
- 1 tbsp (15 mL) **Basil Oil** or olive oil
- 1 garlic clove, pressed

QUESADILLAS

- 1 cup (250 mL) shredded cooked chicken (6 oz/175 g)
- 1 cup (250 mL) shredded Provolone cheese
- 1 tbsp (15 mL) chopped fresh basil
- 4 6-in. (15-cm) flour tortillas

1. For antipasto relish, chop red peppers and olives using **Food Chopper**. Thinly slice pepperoncini and chop all basil using **Utility Knife**; set aside 1 tbsp (15 mL) for quesadillas. Combine red peppers, olives and pepperoncini in **Small Batter Bowl**. Add basil, oil and pressed garlic; mix well and set aside.

2. For quesadillas, shred chicken. Combine chicken, cheese and remaining basil in **Classic Batter Bowl**. Divide chicken mixture among tortillas; fold tortillas in half.

3. To finish quesadillas, lightly brush **Double Burner Griddle** with oil. Heat griddle over medium-high heat 1-3 minutes or until hot. Cook quesadillas 2-3 minutes on each side or until tortillas are golden brown and cheese is melted.

4. To serve, spoon 1 tbsp (15 mL) of the antipasto relish into each quesadilla. Serve with additional relish, if desired.

Yield: 2 servings

U.S. Nutrients per serving (2 quesadillas and 2 tbsp/30 mL relish): Calories 570, Total Fat 29 g, Saturated Fat 12 g, Cholesterol 130 mg, Carbohydrate 33 g, Protein 43 g, Sodium 1100 mg, Fiber 0 g

U.S. Diabetic exchanges per serving: 2 starch, 5 medium-fat meat, 1 fat (2 carb)

CHEF'S CORNER

It is easy to create your own antipasto relish with jarred and bottled condiments available in the grocery store. Jarred roasted red peppers and pepperoncini peppers should have bright, vibrant colors. If your supermarket has an "olive bar," where you can pick and chose the olives you wish to purchase, select kalamata olives that have a dark eggplant color and are plump and juicy.

The extra antipasto relish can be stored, tightly wrapped, in the refrigerator for up to 1 week. It is delicious on sandwiches, pasta or with pita chips.

Folding each tortilla in half to form a crescent shape makes turning quesadillas easier.

20 minutes

THAI BASIL CHICKEN LETTUCE WRAPS

Bottled poppy seed salad dressing gets the flavorful peanut sauce off to a running start for these refreshing wraps.

PEANUT SAUCE

- 2 tbsp (30 mL) dry-roasted peanuts
- 1 tbsp (15 mL) chopped fresh basil
- ¼ cup (50 mL) poppy seed salad dressing
- 2 tsp (10 mL) **Asian Seasoning Mix**
- 1 tbsp (15 mL) rice vinegar
- 1 tbsp (15 mL) water

SALAD

- 1 small cucumber
- ½ medium red bell pepper
- 1½ cups (375 mL) shredded cooked chicken (8 oz/250 g)
- 4 large Boston or bibb lettuce leaves
- Additional chopped peanuts and chopped fresh basil (optional)

1. For sauce, chop peanuts using **Food Chopper**. Chop basil using **Chef's Knife**. Combine peanuts, basil, dressing, seasoning mix, vinegar and water in **Small Batter Bowl**; set aside.

2. For salad, peel cucumber; slice into julienne strips using **Julienne Peeler**, avoiding seeds. Slice bell pepper into thin strips. Shred chicken; toss with half of the sauce. Set remaining sauce aside for dipping.

3. To serve, divide cucumber among lettuce leaves. Spoon chicken mixture over cucumber. Top with bell pepper. Garnish wraps with additional peanuts and basil, if desired. Serve with remaining peanut sauce.

Yield: 2 servings

U.S. Nutrients per serving: Calories 410, Total Fat 22 g, Saturated Fat 5 g, Cholesterol 100 mg, Carbohydrate 13 g, Protein 36 g, Sodium 420 mg, Fiber 2 g

U.S. Diabetic exchanges per serving: 1 starch, 4 low-fat meat, 2 fat (1 carb)

CHEF'S CORNER

These wraps are colorful when served open-face but can also be wrapped between two lettuce leaves, if desired. Romaine, green or red leaf lettuces are also good options for making lettuce wraps.

Tortillas can be substituted for the lettuce leaves for a heartier version.

Our Asian Seasoning Mix gives this peanut sauce the perfect balance of authentic flavor. The sauce can easily be doubled and is delicious served with grilled chicken or with vegetables for dipping.

If desired, 2 tsp (10 mL) soy sauce, 1 tsp (5 mL) finely grated gingerroot and 1 pressed garlic clove can be substituted for the Asian Seasoning Mix.

20 minutes

fish &
seafood

Shrimp Orzo Skillet, p. 61

SESAME TILAPIA WITH SHIITAKE BROTH

Flavorful, pan-fried tilapia becomes a Japanese-inspired one-bowl meal with rice and a gingery mushroom broth.

TILAPIA

- ½ cup (125 mL) panko crumbs
- 1 tbsp (15 mL) sesame seeds
- 1 egg
- 2 boneless, skinless tilapia fillets (4 oz/125 g each)
- 3 tbsp (45 mL) **Asian Seasoning Mix**
- 2 tbsp (30 mL) vegetable oil

SHIITAKE BROTH AND RICE

- 1 small carrot
- 1 green onion with top
- ½ cup (125 mL) sliced shiitake mushrooms
- 1 3-in. (7.5-cm) piece fresh gingerroot, divided
- 2 cups (500 mL) chicken broth
- 1 tbsp (15 mL) reduced-sodium soy sauce
- 1 cup (250 mL) hot cooked white rice

1. For tilapia, combine panko crumbs and sesame seeds in **Coating Tray**. Lightly beat egg in second tray. Cut each fillet into three pieces with **Boning Knife** (see Chef's Corner). Coat tilapia with seasoning mix. Dip each piece into egg and then into panko mixture. Set aside.

2. For broth, peel carrot; cut into julienne strips using **Julienne Peeler**. Thinly slice green onion on a bias. Slice mushrooms. Peel gingerroot; grate 1 tsp (5 mL) of the gingerroot using **Microplane® Adjustable Grater**. Cut remaining gingerroot into ¼-in. (6-mm) slices. Combine carrot, green onion, mushrooms, grated and sliced gingerroot, broth and soy sauce in **(1.5-qt./1.5-L) Saucepan**; bring to a boil.

3. As broth comes to a boil, add oil to **(10-in./25-cm) Skillet**; heat over medium heat 1-3 minutes or until shimmering. Carefully arrange tilapia in Skillet and cook 2-3 minutes or until browned. Turn tilapia over; cook 2-3 minutes or until tilapia flakes easily with a fork, turning with **Small Slotted Turner**.

4. For each serving, pack rice into **Prep Bowl** and invert into bottom of serving bowl. Ladle broth and vegetables around rice; place tilapia over rice.

Yield: 2 servings

U.S. Nutrients per serving: Calories 620, Total Fat 21 g, Saturated Fat 2.5 g, Cholesterol 160 mg, Carbohydrate 72 g, Protein 33 g, Sodium 1070 mg, Fiber 5 g

U.S. Diabetic exchanges per serving: 4 starch, 1 vegetable, 3 medium-fat meat, 1 fat (4 carb)

CHEF'S CORNER

Fresh shiitake mushrooms can be purchased whole or sliced. When using whole mushrooms, remove and discard tough stems before slicing.

To cut tilapia into three equal pieces, slice fillet down center into two portions. Then, cut the thicker portion on an angle into two pieces. This will ensure even cooking.

Panko (PAHN-ko) crumbs are coarse, Japanese-style bread crumbs that are made with crustless bread. These crumbs lend a light coating to the tilapia.

This recipe saves you time by starting with cooked white rice. Freeze small batches of leftover rice in resealable plastic freezer bags for meals like this one.

29 minutes

SHRIMP PANZANELLA SALAD

Using cooked shrimp makes this updated Italian-style bread salad faster to prepare. A lemony vinaigrette adds a fresh twist.

SALAD

- 4 slices (1-in./2.5-cm thick) Italian bread
- 1 tbsp plus ¼ cup (15 mL plus 50 mL) olive oil, divided
- 1 medium carrot
- 1 stalk celery
- 1 lb (500 g) frozen medium cooked shrimp (26-30 per pound), thawed

DRESSING

- 1 lemon
- 2 tbsp (30 mL) snipped fresh parsley
- 1 garlic clove, pressed
- ½ tsp (2 mL) salt
- ¼ tsp (1 mL) coarsely ground black pepper

1. For salad, heat **Grill Pan** over medium-high heat 5 minutes. Lightly brush bread slices with 1 tbsp (15 mL) of the oil using **Chef's Silicone Basting Brush**.

2. As pan heats, peel carrot; cut in half lengthwise, then crosswise on a bias into thin slices. Thinly slice celery on a bias; set carrot and celery aside.

3. Grill bread slices 1-2 minutes on each side or until grill marks appear, turning with **Chef's Tongs**. Remove bread slices from pan and cool on **Cutting Board**. Cut bread slices into cubes with **Bread Knife**.

4. Meanwhile, for dressing, zest lemon to measure 1 tbsp (15 mL) zest. Juice lemon to measure 2 tbsp (30 mL) juice. Snip parsley using **Kitchen Shears**. Whisk together lemon zest, juice, parsley, pressed garlic, salt and black pepper in **Stainless (4-qt./4-L) Mixing Bowl**. Slowly add remaining ¼ cup (50 mL) oil, whisking until well blended.

5. To assemble salad, peel shrimp; remove tails. Add shrimp, carrot and celery to dressing. Fold bread cubes into mixture and serve immediately.

Yield: 4 servings

U.S. Nutrients per serving: Calories 330, Total Fat 19 g, Saturated Fat 2.5 g, Cholesterol 65 mg, Carbohydrate 19 g, Protein 21 g, Sodium 1020 mg, Fiber 2 g

U.S. Diabetic exchanges per serving: 1 starch, 3 medium-fat meat, ½ fat (1 carb)

CHEF'S CORNER

Grilled bread adds great texture and smoky flavor to this salad. Thick-crusted, chewy types, such as ciabatta, will hold up well to the dressing.

Using cooked frozen shrimp saves time. Thawing shrimp overnight in refrigerator is the best. If you don't have time to thaw overnight, place into a bowl of cold water. Drain and pat dry when ready to use. For even faster preparation, buy already peeled shrimp.

This is a great recipe to showcase a high-quality, extra-virgin olive oil. The color and flavor will shine and complement the salad.

24 minutes

PEPPERY FISH CHOWDER

Cooking the potatoes in the microwave oven gives this satisfying soup
a jump-start.

- 2 medium red potatoes
- 1½ cups (375 mL) water, divided
- 1½ tsp (7 mL) salt, divided
- 3 slices peppered bacon
- 1 small onion
- 2 garlic cloves, pressed
- 3 tbsp (45 mL) all-purpose flour

- 2 cups (500 mL) clam juice
- 1 tsp (5 mL) coarsely ground black pepper
- 1 lb (500 g) boneless, skinless tilapia fillets
- ¼ cup (50 mL) snipped fresh parsley
- ½ cup (125 mL) heavy whipping cream
  Hot sauce (optional)

1. Dice potatoes using **Santoku Knife**. Place potatoes, ½ cup (125 mL) of the water and ½ tsp (2 mL) of the salt into **Large Micro-Cooker®**. Cover; microwave on HIGH 6-8 minutes or until tender. Remove from microwave; do not drain.

2. Meanwhile, dice bacon into ½-in. (1-cm) pieces and chop onion. Place bacon into **(4-qt./4-L) Casserole**. Cook over medium heat 5-7 minutes or until crisp. Remove half of the bacon and set aside.

3. Add onion and pressed garlic to remaining bacon in Casserole. Cook 2-3 minutes or until onion is tender. Add flour and cook 1 minute, stirring constantly, until flour is evenly distributed. Slowly add clam juice, potatoes with cooking water, remaining 1 cup (250 mL) water, remaining 1 tsp (5 mL) salt and black pepper; bring to a boil over medium-high heat. Reduce heat to medium and simmer 3-5 minutes.

4. As soup simmers, carefully remove dark reddish brown vein down length of tilapia with **Boning Knife**. Cut tilapia into ¾-in. (2-cm) pieces and add to Casserole. Cook an additional 1-2 minutes or until tilapia is opaque throughout.

5. Meanwhile, snip parsley using **Kitchen Shears**. Remove soup from heat. Stir in cream and parsley and ladle into bowls. Top each serving with reserved bacon pieces. Serve with hot sauce, if desired.

Yield: 4 servings

U.S. Nutrients per serving: Calories 380, Total Fat 20 g, Saturated Fat 10 g, Cholesterol 110 mg, Carbohydrate 25 g, Protein 27 g, Sodium 1330 mg, Fiber 2 g

U.S. Diabetic exchanges per serving: 1½ starch, 3 low-fat meat, 2 fat (1½ carb)

CHEF'S CORNER

Tilapia is a white fish with a mild, slightly sweet flavor. For this soup, it is nice to remove the dark reddish brown vein down the center of each fillet before dicing.

Any firm, white-fleshed fish such as cod or halibut can be substituted for the tilapia, if desired.

You can easily find peppered bacon at a butcher shop. Regular or thick-cut bacon can be substituted for the peppered bacon, if desired. Increase coarsely ground black pepper by ¼ tsp (1 mL).

A roux (ROO) is a mixture of flour and fat that, after being slowly cooked over low heat, is used to thicken mixtures such as soups and sauces.

25 minutes

DIJON-CRUSTED HALIBUT AND ROASTED ASPARAGUS

Save precious time by roasting halibut and asparagus simultaneously in the same pan. For easy clean-up, line the pan with Parchment Paper.

2 slices French bread

1 tbsp (15 mL) snipped fresh parsley

1 tbsp plus 1 tsp (15 mL plus 5 mL)
   Garlic Oil or olive oil, divided

¼ cup (50 mL) Dijon mustard

1 garlic clove, pressed

½ tsp (2 mL) salt

¼ tsp (1 mL) coarsely ground black pepper

4 boneless, skinless halibut fillets
   (4 oz/125 g each)

1 lb (500 g) asparagus spears

   Additional Garlic Oil, salt and coarsely
   ground black pepper

1. Preheat oven to 450°F (230°C). Chop bread using **Food Chopper**. Snip parsley using **Kitchen Shears**. Combine bread crumbs and 1 tbsp (15 mL) of the oil in **Small Micro-Cooker®**. Microwave on HIGH 1 minute or until bread crumbs are light golden brown and crisp, stirring after 30 seconds. Cool slightly and stir in parsley.

2. Whisk mustard, pressed garlic, salt, black pepper and remaining 1 tsp (5 mL) oil in **Stainless (2-qt./2-L) Mixing Bowl**. Place halibut on **Large Bar Pan**; spread 1 tbsp (15 mL) of the mustard mixture evenly onto each fillet. Press bread crumbs onto mustard mixture.

3. Trim asparagus (see Chef's Corner). Cut asparagus in half crosswise and brush with additional oil; season with salt and black pepper. Arrange asparagus next to halibut in a single layer on bar pan. Bake 11-13 minutes or until halibut flakes easily with a fork and crust is golden brown.

Yield: 4 servings

U.S. Nutrients per serving: Calories 270, Total Fat 12 g, Saturated Fat 1 g, Cholesterol 35 mg, Carbohydrate 14 g, Protein 28 g, Sodium 890 mg, Fiber 3 g

U.S. Diabetic exchanges per serving: 1 starch, 3½ low-fat meat (1 carb)

CHEF'S CORNER

The Food Chopper makes quick work of a small amount of bread, which adds a light crunch to the topping.

Roasting the halibut and asparagus side by side at the same time makes the most of your oven and saves time. Heating the oven at 450°F (230°C) cooks the halibut through, while giving the asparagus a nice caramelization.

Trim asparagus to avoid tough ends. First, line up the asparagus spears, aligning tips. Trim bottom 1 in. (2.5 cm) so spears are the same length; discard ends. Then, use a **Vegetable Peeler** to peel off the tough skin from the bottom 1 in. (2.5 cm) of each spear.

18 minutes

SAKE-GLAZED HALIBUT WITH EDAMAME RICE

Sake is reduced with prepared teriyaki basting sauce to make a thick, flavorful glaze. Brushing some of the glaze onto the halibut before broiling results in an intense caramelized flavor.

GLAZE AND HALIBUT

- 1 tsp (5 mL) grated fresh gingerroot
- 1 cup (250 mL) sake (see Chef's Corner)
- ½ cup (125 mL) teriyaki baste and glaze
- 2 boneless, skinless halibut fillets (4 oz/125 g each)

EDAMAME RICE

- 1 green onion with top
- 1 cup (250 mL) hot cooked white rice
- ½ cup (125 mL) frozen shelled edamame beans, thawed
- ¼ cup (50 mL) prepared glaze (see left)

1. Preheat broiler on HIGH. For glaze, grate gingerroot using **Microplane® Adjustable Grater**. Combine gingerroot, sake and teriyaki baste and glaze in **(1.5-qt./1.5-L) Saucepan**. Bring to a simmer over medium-high heat; cook, stirring occasionally, 7-9 minutes or until mixture coats the back of a spoon and is reduced by half. Remove from heat and cool slightly. Set aside 2 tbsp (30 mL) glaze for halibut. (Reserve remaining glaze for later use.)

2. Place halibut in **Stainless (8-in./20-cm) Sauté Pan** (do not use nonstick cookware) and brush top evenly with reserved 2 tbsp (30 mL) glaze. Broil 8-10 minutes or until halibut flakes easily with a fork and glaze is brown and blistered.

3. As halibut cooks, prepare rice. Slice green onion using **Santoku Knife**. Combine green onion, rice, edamame and ¼ cup (50 mL) of the remaining glaze in **Small Micro-Cooker®** (reserve remaining glaze for serving); microwave on HIGH 2-3 minutes or until heated through, stirring after 1 minute.

4. To serve, divide rice among serving plates; top with halibut. Drizzle remaining glaze over halibut and around edge of plate.

Yield: 2 servings

Light • U.S. Nutrients per serving: Calories 550, Total Fat 4 g, Saturated Fat 0 g, Cholesterol 35 mg, Carbohydrate 57 g, Protein 34 g, Sodium 1690 mg, Fiber 5 g

U.S. Diabetic exchanges per serving: 3 starch, ½ fruit, 3½ low-fat meat (3½ carb)

CHEF'S CORNER

Sake (SAH-keh) is a Japanese wine made from fermented rice. Once opened, it will keep, tightly sealed in the refrigerator for at least 3 weeks.

There's no need to purchase the most expensive sake available, since it will be heated and mixed with other ingredients.

This recipe saves you time by starting with cooked white rice. Freeze small batches of leftover rice in resealable plastic freezer bags for meals like this one.

To make your own baste and glaze, combine ½ cup (125 mL) thin teriyaki sauce, ¼ cup (50 mL) cold water and 1 tbsp (15 mL) cornstarch in (1.5-qt./1.5-L) Saucepan. Bring to a boil, whisking constantly until thickened.

Salmon or cod can be substituted for the halibut, if desired.

26 minutes

CRISPY PARMESAN SHRIMP WITH SPAGHETTI

The innovative technique of creating Parmesan crisps in a skillet gives these shrimp a crunchy coating without frying them.

3 oz (90 g) Parmesan cheese
1 egg white
1 garlic clove, pressed
¼ tsp (1 mL) salt
½ tsp (2 mL) coarsely ground black pepper

1 lb (500 g) frozen large uncooked shrimp (21-25 per pound), thawed
2 tbsp (30 mL) snipped fresh parsley
8 oz (250 mL) uncooked spaghetti
2 cups (500 mL) broccoli florets
1 cup (250 mL) marinara sauce

1. Preheat oven to 425°F (220°C). To start pasta, bring salted water to a boil in **(4-qt./4-L) Casserole**.

2. Meanwhile, for Parmesan topping, lightly spray *nonstick* **(12-in./30-cm) Skillet** (see Chef's Corner) with vegetable oil using **Kitchen Spritzer**; heat over medium heat 1-3 minutes or until hot. Grate cheese evenly over bottom of Skillet using **Deluxe Cheese Grater** fitted with coarse grating drum. Cook 4-5 minutes or until cheese is lacy and golden. Starting at edges, immediately loosen cheese with **Small Slotted Turner**; slide onto cutting board and cool completely. Place cheese crisp into resealable plastic bag; coarsely crush into crumbs using flat side of **Meat Tenderizer**.

3. For shrimp, whisk together egg white, pressed garlic, salt and black pepper in **Classic Batter Bowl**. Peel and devein shrimp; remove tails. Add shrimp to egg mixture and toss to coat. Arrange shrimp in a single layer in **Deep Dish Baker**.

4. Snip parsley with **Kitchen Shears** and toss with cheese crumbs. Sprinkle cheese mixture over shrimp. Bake 10-12 minutes or until shrimp are cooked through.

5. Add pasta to boiling water; cook 4 minutes. Meanwhile, cut broccoli into small florets and add to boiling pasta; cook 1-2 minutes or until pasta is cooked to desired tenderness.

6. Meanwhile, place sauce into **Small Micro-Cooker®** and microwave on HIGH 2-3 minutes or until heated through. Drain pasta and broccoli. To serve, divide pasta mixture among serving plates. Spoon sauce over pasta mixture; top with shrimp.

Yield: 4 servings

Light • U.S. Nutrients per serving: Calories 430, Total Fat 11 g, Saturated Fat 4 g, Cholesterol 85 mg, Carbohydrate 49 g, Protein 37 g, Sodium 1250 mg, Fiber 4 g

U.S. Diabetic exchanges per serving: 3 starch, 4 low-fat meat (3 carb)

CHEF'S CORNER

When preparing the Parmesan topping, the cheese will melt and turn lacy before turning golden light brown. It is important to use nonstick cookware for this recipe; the cheese will stick in other types of cookware. Remove the cheese as soon as it comes off heat so that it can cool quickly.

Other types of hard Italian cheeses like Asiago can be substituted for the Parmesan cheese, if desired.

29 minutes

GARAM MASALA SALMON

A popular spice blend in India, garam masala adds an authentic, subtly spicy flavor that warmly complements salmon's distinctive flavor.

RAITA

- 2 tsp (10 mL) grated fresh gingerroot
- 1 lemon
- ¾ cup (175 mL) plain yogurt
- 1 garlic clove, pressed
- ⅛ tsp (0.5 mL) ground cumin
- ¼ tsp (1 mL) salt
- 1 tbsp (15 mL) snipped fresh cilantro

SALMON AND ZUCCHINI

- 2 boneless, skinless salmon fillets
  (4 oz/125 g each)
- ¼ tsp (1 mL) salt
- 2 tsp (10 mL) olive oil
- ½ tsp (2 mL) garam masala spice blend
  (see Chef's Corner)
- 3 small zucchini

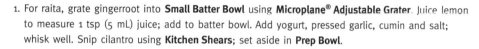

1. For raita, grate gingerroot into **Small Batter Bowl** using **Microplane® Adjustable Grater**. Juice lemon to measure 1 tsp (5 mL) juice; add to batter bowl. Add yogurt, pressed garlic, cumin and salt; whisk well. Snip cilantro using **Kitchen Shears**; set aside in **Prep Bowl**.

2. For salmon, season salmon with salt; place into **Stainless (2-qt./2-L) Mixing Bowl** with ¼ cup (50 mL) of the raita, turning to coat.

3. As salmon marinates, add oil and garam masala to **(10-in./25-cm) Sauté Pan**; heat over medium heat 1-2 minutes or until fragrant. Add salmon (discard marinade); cook 3-4 minutes or until browned. Turn salmon over; cook 3-4 minutes or until salmon flakes easily with a fork.

4. Meanwhile, cut zucchini lengthwise into long ribbons using **Vegetable Peeler**, avoiding seeds.

5. To serve, place salmon and zucchini ribbons onto serving plates. Stir cilantro into remaining raita and drizzle over zucchini just before serving.

Yield: 2 servings

U.S. Nutrients per serving: Calories 340, Total Fat 19 g, Saturated Fat 4 g, Cholesterol 70 mg, Carbohydrate 14 g, Protein 30 g, Sodium 730 mg, Fiber 2 g

U.S. Diabetic exchanges per serving: ½ milk, 1 vegetable, 3½ medium-fat meat (½ carb)

CHEF'S CORNER

Toasting the garam masala in oil brings out the flavors in the blend because it releases the oils in the spices, further enhancing the flavor of the salmon.

Garam masala is an Indian spice blend that includes spices such as cinnamon, cloves, cardamom and mace. Garam masala can be purchased in Indian markets and in the spice section of most supermarkets.

Raitas are yogurt-based sauces that often include chopped vegetables, spices and herbs. They are designed to be a cooling counterbalance for many spicy Indian dishes.

18 minutes

RIGATONI WITH TUNA AND SUN-DRIED TOMATOES

Tossing the pasta in the Stir-Fry Skillet with the other ingredients lightly sauces the pasta while delivering a lot of flavor.

8 oz (250 g) uncooked rigatoni pasta	1 lemon
2 oz (60 g) Parmesan cheese, divided	3 tbsp (45 mL) olive oil
½ cup (125 mL) sun-dried tomatoes packed in oil, drained	2 garlic cloves, pressed
½ cup (125 mL) chopped fresh parsley, divided	½ tsp (2 mL) crushed red pepper flakes
	1 pouch (7.06 oz/200 g) chunk light tuna

1. Bring salted water to a boil in **(4-qt./4-L) Casserole**. Cook pasta according to package directions; drain.

2. Meanwhile, grate cheese using **Deluxe Cheese Grater**. Pat tomatoes dry using paper towels. Slice tomatoes and chop parsley using **Santoku Knife**. Cut lemon into wedges; set aside.

3. Heat oil, pressed garlic and pepper flakes in **Stir-Fry Skillet** over medium-high heat 1-2 minutes or until garlic turns golden (do not allow to burn). Immediately stir in tuna and tomatoes; cook 2-3 minutes or until tomatoes are tender. Add pasta, half of the parsley and half of the cheese to Skillet; toss gently.

4. To serve, divide pasta among serving plates. Sprinkle with remaining parsley and cheese. Serve with lemon wedges.

Yield: 4 servings

U.S. Nutrients per serving: Calories 450, Total Fat 16 g, Saturated Fat 5 g, Cholesterol 30 mg, Carbohydrate 48 g, Protein 27 g, Sodium 370 mg, Fiber 3 g

U.S. Diabetic exchanges per serving: 3 starch, 1 vegetable, 1 medium-fat meat, 1 fat (3 carb)

CHEF'S CORNER

Sun-dried tomatoes are vine-ripened tomatoes that have been picked and dried. These tomatoes deliver an intense flavor year round. Sun-dried tomatoes can be purchased dried or oil-packed.

This recipe is great with traditional Italian tuna, or *tonno*, which has a rich, mellow flavor. Look for olive oil-packed tuna in the gourmet or Italian section of larger supermarkets.

Canned tuna can be substituted for the vacuum-packed tuna.

To round out the meal, serve with a fresh arugula salad tossed with red wine vinaigrette.

25 minutes

SHRIMP ORZO SKILLET

Quick-cooking shrimp are a mainstay in busy kitchens. Orzo is another staple that cooks faster than rice. Both orzo and shrimp cook in the same Skillet for this recipe.

SHRIMP

- 8 oz (250 g) large uncooked shrimp (21-25 per pound)
- 1 tbsp (15 mL) vegetable oil
- ¼ tsp (1 mL) salt
- ¼ tsp (1 mL) coarsely ground black pepper
- ⅛ tsp (0.5 mL) sugar (see Chef's Corner)

ORZO

- 8 oz (250 g) orzo pasta
- 1 garlic clove, pressed
- 2 cups (500 mL) chicken broth
- 1 cup (250 mL) clam juice
- 1 lemon
- 1 tbsp (15 mL) thinly sliced fresh mint
- 1 cup (250 mL) frozen peas
- 1 tbsp (15 mL) butter

CHEF'S CORNER

The small amount of sugar that is added to the shrimp promotes caramelization in the short time that it takes to cook the shrimp.

To slice mint into thin ribbons, use a technique called chiffonade (shif-uh-NAHD). Stack mint leaves on top of each other and roll into a tight cylinder. Slice crosswise using Santoku Knife; separate into ribbons.

Blanched asparagus spears, cut into 1-in. (2.5-cm) pieces can be substituted for the peas, if desired.

Orzo is a tiny, rice-shaped pasta that is great in soups and wonderful as a substitute for rice.

1. For shrimp, peel and devein shrimp. Add oil to **(10-in./25-cm) Skillet**; heat over medium-high heat 1-3 minutes or until shimmering. As Skillet heats, combine salt, black pepper and sugar in **Small Batter Bowl**; add shrimp and toss to coat.

2. Arrange shrimp in a single layer over bottom of Skillet and cook about 1 minute or until one side is browned and edges are pink. Remove Skillet from heat and turn shrimp over with **Small Slotted Turner**; let stand an additional 30 seconds or until centers are opaque and shrimp is cooked through. Remove shrimp from Skillet, set aside.

3. For orzo, in same Skillet, combine orzo, pressed garlic, broth and clam juice. Bring to a boil; cover and reduce heat to medium-low. Cook 10-12 minutes or until orzo is cooked through.

4. As orzo cooks, zest lemon with **Microplane® Adjustable Grater** to measure 1 tbsp (15 mL) zest; juice lemon to measure 1 tbsp (15 mL) juice. Thinly slice mint using **Santoku Knife**.

5. Remove Skillet from heat and stir in peas, butter and lemon juice. Arrange shrimp over orzo; cover and let stand 3-5 minutes or until heated through. Sprinkle with lemon zest and mint before serving.

Yield: 4 servings

Light • U.S. Nutrients per serving: Calories 330, Total Fat 8 g, Saturated Fat 2 g, Cholesterol 40 mg, Carbohydrate 49 g, Protein 19 g, Sodium 840 mg, Fiber 4 g

U.S. Diabetic exchanges per serving: 3½ starch, 1 low-fat meat (3½ carb)

29 minutes

GRILLED TILAPIA WITH PINEAPPLE SALSA

Taco seasoning mix gives a flavor boost with minimum effort. As the tilapia cooks, you can prepare the flavorful salsa.

PINEAPPLE SALSA

- ½ medium pineapple
- ¼ small red onion
- 1 serrano pepper
- 2 tbsp (30 mL) chopped fresh cilantro
- ⅛ tsp (0.5 mL) salt
- 1 lime

TILAPIA

- 1 packet (1.25 oz/35 g) taco seasoning mix
- 3 tbsp (45 mL) **Garlic Oil** or olive oil
- 4 boneless, skinless tilapia fillets (about 4 oz/125 g each)

1. Heat **Grill Pan** over medium-high heat 5 minutes. As pan heats, using **Santoku Knife**, peel pineapple half; cut lengthwise into two pieces and remove core. Slice each pineapple piece lengthwise into three strips. Arrange strips in a single layer over Grill Pan; cook 2-3 minutes on each side or until grill marks appear. Set aside on **Cutting Board**.

2. While pineapple cooks, chop onion. Cut serrano pepper lengthwise in half; remove and discard seeds. Chop serrano pepper and cilantro. Combine onion, serrano pepper, cilantro and salt in **Small Batter Bowl**. Zest lime using **Microplane® Adjustable Grater** to measure 1 tsp (5 mL) zest. Juice lime to measure 1 tbsp (15 mL) juice. Add zest and juice to batter bowl; mix well.

3. Whisk taco seasoning mix and oil in **Stainless (4-qt./4-L) Mixing Bowl**. Add tilapia; turn to coat. Place two tilapia fillets onto Grill Pan. Cook 2 minutes or until grill marks appear. Turn tilapia over using **Jumbo Slotted Turner**; cook 2 minutes or until tilapia flakes easily with a fork. Remove tilapia from pan. Wipe out pan and repeat with remaining fillets.

4. As tilapia cooks, chop pineapple and add to onion mixture in batter bowl; mix well. To serve, top tilapia with pineapple salsa.

Yield: 4 servings

U.S. Nutrients per serving: Calories 240, Total Fat 12 g, Saturated Fat 1.5 g, Cholesterol 55 mg, Carbohydrate 13 g, Protein 23 g, Sodium 780 mg, Fiber 2 g

U.S. Diabetic exchanges per serving: 1 fruit, 3 low-fat meat, ½ fat (1 carb)

CHEF'S CORNER

To save time, buy peeled and cored pineapple from the refrigerated section of your produce department.

If desired, 1 can (20 oz/398 g) pineapple slices in juice can be substituted for the fresh pineapple. Pat pineapple slices dry with paper towels before cooking to promote grill marks.

25 minutes

BARBECUE SALMON WITH RADISH SLAW

Reducing cider vinegar and honey creates an intensely flavored glaze for the salmon that is also used as dressing for a zesty slaw.

½ cup (125 mL) cider vinegar

⅓ cup (75 mL) honey

1 lb (500 g) radishes (about 3 cups/ 750 mL)

1 medium carrot

2 tbsp (30 mL) snipped fresh parsley

4 skinless salmon fillets (4 oz/125 g each)

2 tbsp (30 mL) **Smoky Barbecue Rub**

½ tsp (2 mL) salt

½ tsp (2 mL) coarsely ground black pepper

1 tbsp (15 mL) olive oil

1. Pour vinegar into **Small Batter Bowl**. Microwave on HIGH 4 minutes or until reduced by half. Whisk in honey; microwave an additional 3-4 minutes or until beginning to thicken. Using **Oven Mitts**, carefully remove batter bowl from microwave; set aside to cool. (Honey mixture will be very hot.)

2. Meanwhile, slice radishes using **Ultimate Mandoline** fitted with v-shaped blade. Cut slices into thin julienne strips with **Santoku Knife** (see Chef's Corner). Peel carrot; cut into julienne strips using **Julienne Peeler**. Snip parsley using **Kitchen Shears**. Combine radishes, carrot and parsley in **Classic Batter Bowl**.

3. Heat **Grill Pan** over medium-high heat 5 minutes. As pan heats, coat salmon on all sides with barbecue rub. Cook 2-3 minutes or until grill marks appear. Turn salmon over; cook 2-3 minutes or until salmon flakes easily with a fork. Remove from heat. Pour 3 tbsp (45 mL) of the honey mixture into **Prep Bowl** and brush over salmon.

4. To serve, whisk salt and black pepper into remaining honey mixture. Slowly add oil while whisking constantly until blended. Pour vinaigrette over radish mixture; toss to coat. Serve slaw immediately with salmon.

Yield: 4 servings

U.S. Nutrients per serving: Calories 360, Total Fat 16 g, Saturated Fat 3 g, Cholesterol 65 mg, Carbohydrate 31 g, Protein 24 g, Sodium 640 mg, Fiber less than 1 g

U.S. Diabetic exchanges per serving: 2 fruit, 3 medium-fat meat (2 carb)

CHEF'S CORNER

The Ultimate Mandoline quickly and evenly slices radishes. To easily cut slices into julienne strips, arrange slices in a long row before cutting crosswise.

To check for bones in salmon fillet, bend raw fillet back and run fingers over surface of fillet. You can easily pull out any pin bones with your fingers.

Reducing the vinegar evaporates the water and intensifies the flavor.

23 minutes

CAMPANELLE WITH CREAMY TOMATO-CLAM SAUCE

Enhancing a jarred vodka sauce cuts down significantly on time and ingredients. A crunchy bread crumb topping adds great texture to the finished dish.

PASTA AND TOPPING

- 8 oz (250 g) uncooked campanelle pasta
- 2 slices French bread
- 2 tbsp (30 mL) snipped fresh parsley
- 1 tbsp (15 mL) butter

SAUCE

- 2 cans (6½ oz/190 g each) minced clams, undrained
- 1 cup (250 mL) jarred vodka marinara sauce
- 2 garlic cloves, pressed
- 1 lemon

1. Bring salted water to a boil in **(4-qt./4-L) Casserole**. Cook pasta according to package directions. Drain using large **Colander**; set aside.

2. As pasta cooks, prepare topping. Chop bread using **Food Chopper**. Snip parsley using **Kitchen Shears**. Place butter into **(8-in./20-cm) Sauté Pan**; melt over medium heat. Add bread crumbs; stir with **Classic Scraper** 2-3 minutes or until bread crumbs are crisp and golden. Remove pan from heat, cool slightly. Stir in parsley.

3. For sauce, strain clam juice into same Casserole with **Can Strainer**. Add vodka sauce and pressed garlic. Juice lemon to measure 1 tbsp (15 mL) juice; stir into sauce. Bring to a simmer over medium heat. Remove from heat and stir in pasta and clams; cover and let stand 3-5 minutes or until heated through.

4. To serve, divide pasta among serving plates; sprinkle with bread crumb mixture.

Yield: 4 servings

Light • U.S. Nutrients per serving: Calories 380, Total Fat 9 g, Saturated Fat 4 g, Cholesterol 35 mg, Carbohydrate 57 g, Protein 17 g, Sodium 1070 mg, Fiber 3 g

U.S. Diabetic exchanges per serving: 4 starch, 1 low-fat meat (4 carb)

CHEF'S CORNER

Homemade toasted bread crumbs are a deliciously easy way to finish a dish. Always use fresh bread and make sure the butter is hot and bubbly before adding the crumbs so that the finished crumbs will be crisp and golden.

Campanelle is a trumpet-shaped pasta. Other pasta shapes such as rotini or penne can be substituted for the campanelle, if desired.

25 minutes

beef &
pork

Moroccan Pork Chops, p. 99

ULTIMATE PEPPERCORN BURGERS

These bistro-style burgers are designed to be cooked until well-done, yet they are juicy and flavorful. How? A bread "paste" lends incredible moistness.

1 small onion

1 tbsp (15 mL) vegetable oil

2 slices firm white sandwich bread

⅓ cup (75 mL) milk

1 tbsp (15 mL) **Crushed Peppercorn & Garlic Rub**

1 lb (500 g) 85% lean ground beef such as chuck

4 onion rolls, split

Additional toppings such as steak sauce, sliced tomatoes or cooked bacon (optional)

1. Heat **Grill Pan** over medium heat 5 minutes. As pan heats, slice onion crosswise into ½-in. (1-cm) rings using **Chef's Knife**; brush with oil. Cook onion 2-3 minutes on each side or until grill marks appear and onion is tender. Remove from pan; tent with foil and set aside.

2. As onion cooks, remove and discard crusts from bread; tear bread into pieces. Combine bread, milk and peppercorn rub in **Stainless (4-qt./4-L) Mixing Bowl**. Mix until a smooth paste forms. Sprinkle ground beef over bread paste and mix gently until incorporated.

3. Form meat mixture into four thin patties, about 4 in. (10 cm) in diameter. Grill patties 3-4 minutes or until grill marks appear. Turn patties over using **Jumbo Slotted Turner**; cook 3-4 minutes or until internal temperature reaches 160°F (71°C) and patties are no longer pink in center. Transfer burgers to paper towel-lined plate.

4. To serve, place burgers in rolls. Top with onions and serve with additional toppings, if desired.

Yield: 4 servings

U.S. Nutrients per serving: Calories 510, Total Fat 24 g, Saturated Fat 8 g, Cholesterol 80 mg, Carbohydrate 42 g, Protein 29 g, Sodium 890 mg, Fiber 2 g

U.S. Diabetic exchanges per serving: 3 starch, 3 medium-fat meat, 1 fat (3 carb)

CHEF'S CORNER

This bread paste is called a *panade* (puh-NAHD) in French, which is a mixture of bread and milk used to bind ground meats. It produces surprisingly juicy well-done burgers.

We recommend using 85% lean ground chuck for best flavor and tenderness. Other types of ground beef such as ground round can be substituted.

To take into account shrinkage during cooking, form patties about ½ in. (2 cm) larger than the diameter of the buns for a perfect fit when serving.

If desired, 3 garlic cloves, pressed, ½ tsp (2 mL) salt and ½ tsp (2 mL) coarsely ground black pepper can be substituted for the peppercorn rub.

21 minutes

CHIMICHURRI STEAK SALAD

Argentina's favorite salsa, chimichurri, doubles as a marinade and salad dressing.

STEAK
- 1 lb (500 g) boneless top sirloin steak, about ¾ in. (2 cm) thick
- ½ tsp (2 mL) salt

CHIMICHURRI SALSA
- 1 cup (250 mL) chopped fresh parsley
- ¼ cup (50 mL) olive oil
- 2 tbsp (30 mL) red wine vinegar
- ½ tsp (2 mL) salt
- 1 garlic clove, pressed
- ¼ tsp (1 mL) ground cayenne pepper

SALAD
- 2 heads romaine hearts (about 8 cups/2 L)
- 1 cup (250 mL) grape tomatoes

1. For steak, heat **Grill Pan** over medium heat 5 minutes. As pan heats, rub steak with salt. Place steak into pan; cook 6-8 minutes or until grill marks appear. Turn steak over and cook an additional 6-8 minutes or until **Pocket Thermometer** registers 155°F (68°C) for medium doneness. Remove from heat; transfer steak to cutting board (temperature will rise to 160°F/71°C).

2. As steak cooks, prepare salsa. Chop parsley with **Food Chopper**. Combine parsley, oil, vinegar, salt, garlic and cayenne pepper in **Small Batter Bowl**. Spoon 3 tbsp (45 mL) salsa evenly over steak. Let stand 10 minutes.

3. While steak stands, prepare salad. Thinly slice lettuce and cut tomatoes in half lengthwise using **Santoku Knife**; place lettuce and tomatoes into large serving bowl. Pour remaining salsa over salad and toss gently.

4. To serve, divide salad among serving plates. Thinly slice steak and arrange over top of salad.

Yield: 4 servings

U.S. Nutrients per serving: Calories 330, Total Fat 22 g, Saturated Fat 5 g, Cholesterol 55 mg, Carbohydrate 7 g, Protein 27 g, Sodium 660 mg, Fiber 2 g

U.S. Diabetic exchanges per serving: 1 vegetable, 3½ medium-fat meat, 1 fat (0 carb)

CHEF'S CORNER
Marinating the steak with the chimichurri salsa *after* cooking infuses the meat with flavor and keeps it moist and tender. In Argentina, where chimichurri originated, the salsa is served with meat, poultry and fish or used as a dipping sauce. Vary the flavor by adding jalapeño peppers or substituting cilantro for the parsley.

When working with sirloin steaks, trim all fat and as much connective tissue around the steaks as possible before cooking.

To serve with grilled garlic bread, see p. 123, Step 1.

27 minutes

BLT MAC & CHEESE

The "L" stands for leeks in this "adult" macaroni and cheese. The pasta, cheeses and seasonings are cooked in the same pot, all at the same time.

5 cups (1.2 L) water

8 slices bacon

4 oz (125 g) sharp white cheddar cheese

1 oz (30 g) Parmesan cheese

4 oz (125 g) cream cheese

1 lb (500 g) uncooked cellentani or cavatappi pasta

1 tsp (5 mL) salt

½ tsp (2 mL) coarsely ground black pepper

1 large leek (white and light green portions only)

3 large plum tomatoes

1. To start pasta mixture, bring water to a boil in **(8-qt./7.6-L) Stockpot**.

2. Meanwhile, slice bacon crosswise into thin strips. Place into **(10-in./25-cm) Skillet**; cook over medium-high heat 8-10 minutes or until crisp. Remove bacon from Skillet to paper towel-lined plate.

3. As bacon cooks, grate cheddar and Parmesan cheeses. Add pasta, cream cheese, grated cheese, salt and black pepper to boiling water in Stockpot. Cover and simmer vigorously 5 minutes, stirring occasionally.

4. As pasta mixture cooks, slice leek in half lengthwise, then crosswise into ½-in. (1-cm) slices. Place into **Small Batter Bowl** and swish in cold water to remove dirt; lift leeks out of water and stir into pasta mixture. Cook, uncovered, 5-7 minutes or until pasta is cooked to desired tenderness and sauce is thickened, stirring occasionally.

5. Meanwhile, cut tomatoes in half lengthwise using **Tomato Knife**; remove cores and scrape out seeds. Dice tomatoes; reserve ¼ cup (50 mL) for garnish. Remove Stockpot from heat; stir in remaining tomatoes and half of the bacon. Spoon pasta mixture into serving bowl and garnish with reserved tomatoes and bacon. Serve immediately.

Yield: 6 servings

U.S. Nutrients per serving: Calories 500, Total Fat 19 g, Saturated Fat 11 g, Cholesterol 50 mg, Carbohydrate 61 g, Protein 21 g, Sodium 820 mg, Fiber 3 g

U.S. Diabetic exchanges per serving: 4 starch, 1 high-fat meat, 2 fat (4 carb)

CHEF'S CORNER

The one-pot technique of boiling the pasta, water and cheeses together creates a creamy, emulsified sauce that adds great flavor to the pasta.

Other shapes of pasta can be substituted for cellentani, if desired. Look for a shape that cooks in 10-12 minutes for best results.

For a heartier dish, add diced cooked chicken, if desired.

24 minutes

BEEF TENDERLOIN WITH MUSHROOM RAGOÛT

This upscale presentation of beef tenderloin features a delicious restaurant-style pan sauce with sautéed mushrooms, shallots and red wine.

BEEF

- 1 tsp (5 mL) olive oil
- 2 beef tenderloin filets (4-6 oz/125-175 g each), cut 1 in. (2.5 cm) thick, trimmed
  Salt and coarsely ground black pepper
  Quick Polenta (see Chef's Corner)

MUSHROOM RAGOÛT

- 2 cups (500 mL) baby portobello or white mushrooms (5 oz/150 g)

- 2 large shallots
- 3/4 cup (75 mL) dry red wine such as Cabernet Sauvignon
- 2 tbsp (30 mL) chopped fresh parsley
- 1/2 cup (125 mL) reduced-sodium beef broth
- 2 tbsp (30 mL) butter
  Salt and coarsely ground black pepper to taste

1. For beef, add oil to **(10-in./25-cm) Skillet**; heat over medium-high heat 1-3 minutes or until shimmering. As pan heats, season both sides of filets with salt and black pepper.

2. Cook filets undisturbed 2-3 minutes or until well browned. Turn filets over; cook an additional 2-3 minutes or until **Pocket Thermometer** registers 140°F (60°C) for medium-rare doneness. Remove from heat; transfer filets to plate and let stand 5 minutes (temperature will rise to 145°F/63°C).

3. As beef cooks, prepare *Quick Polenta* (see Chef's Corner). Meanwhile, start ragoût. Chop mushrooms with **Santoku Knife**. Add mushrooms to Skillet; return Skillet to medium-high heat. Cook 3-4 minutes or until mushrooms are golden brown, stirring occasionally. Remove mushrooms from Skillet.

4. As mushrooms cook, thinly slice shallots; add shallots and wine to Skillet. Simmer 3-4 minutes or until wine is almost completely evaporated. Meanwhile, chop parsley. Add half of the parsley and broth; simmer an additional 1-2 minutes or until broth is reduced by half.

5. Return mushrooms to Skillet and whisk in butter using **Silicone Flat Whisk**. Season sauce to taste with salt and black pepper. To serve, divide polenta between serving plates. Slice beef into thick slices and place over polenta. Top with ragoût and remaining parsley. Serve immediately.

Yield: 2 servings

U.S. Nutrients per serving (including polenta): Calories 560, Total Fat 32 g, Saturated Fat 17 g, Cholesterol 125 mg, Carbohydrate 26 g, Protein 29 g, Sodium 890 mg, Fiber 2 g

U.S. Diabetic exchanges per serving (including polenta): 2 starch, 3 medium-fat meat, 3 fat (2 carb)

CHEF'S CORNER

Traditional polenta is made from coarsely ground cornmeal. A quick version can be made using standard cornmeal. *Quick Polenta*: combine 1 1/2 cups (75 mL) water, 1/4 tsp (1 mL) salt, 1/8 tsp (0.5 mL) coarsely ground black pepper and 1 pressed garlic clove in **Small Micro-Cooker®**; cover and microwave on HIGH 2 minutes or until water is steaming. Whisk in 1/3 cup (175 mL) yellow cornmeal. Microwave 2 minutes. Whisk in 1 tbsp (15 mL) heavy whipping cream and 1 tbsp (15 mL) butter.

For best flavor and texture, be sure to brown the mushrooms well. Remove mushrooms from the Skillet before cooking the shallots and wine.

29 minutes

GREMOLATA STEAK WITH MASCARPONE POTATOES

This Italian-style dish features a zesty combination of lemon, fresh parsley and garlic. Serve with red potatoes mashed with creamy mascarpone cheese.

STEAK

- 1 tsp (5 mL) olive oil
- 1 boneless New York strip or ribeye steak, cut 3/4 in. (2 cm) thick (8-12 oz/250-350 g)
  Salt and coarsely ground black pepper

POTATOES

- 4 small red potatoes
- 1½ cups (375 mL) water
- 2 tbsp (30 mL) mascarpone cheese
- ½ tsp (2 mL) salt

GREMOLATA VINAIGRETTE

- 1 tbsp (15 mL) olive oil
- 1 garlic clove, pressed
- 1 lemon
- 2 tsp (10 mL) finely chopped Italian parsley
- Salt

1. For steak, add oil to **(10-in./25-cm) Skillet**; heat over medium-high heat 1-3 minutes or until shimmering. As pan heats, season both sides of steak with salt and black pepper. Place steak into Skillet; reduce heat to medium and cook undisturbed 3-4 minutes or until browned. Turn steak over and cook an additional 3-4 minutes or until **Pocket Thermometer** registers 155°F (68°C) for medium doneness. Remove from heat; transfer steak to plate and tent with foil (temperature will rise to 160°F/71°C).

2. As steak cooks, prepare potatoes. Cut potatoes into quarters using **Utility Knife**. Place potatoes and water into **Small Micro-Cooker®**; microwave on HIGH 8-10 minutes or until tender. Drain water; carefully remove lid and add cheese and salt. Mash potatoes using **Mix 'N Masher**; cover and set aside.

3. As potatoes cook, prepare vinaigrette. Wipe out Skillet and add oil. Press garlic into Skillet; heat over medium-low heat 30 seconds or until garlic is fragrant (do not brown). Remove garlic mixture from heat and pour into **Small Batter Bowl**. Zest entire lemon using **Microplane® Adjustable Grater**. Juice lemon with **Citrus Press** to measure 1 tbsp (15 mL) juice and add to batter bowl. Chop parsley using **Santoku Knife**. Add lemon zest and parsley to batter bowl; mix well and season to taste with salt.

4. To serve, divide potatoes between serving plates. Cut steak in half and place one half onto each plate. Drizzle steak with vinaigrette and serve.

Yield: 2 servings

U.S. Nutrients per serving: Calories 570, Total Fat 45 g, Saturated Fat 17 g, Cholesterol 110 mg, Carbohydrate 20 g, Protein 26 g, Sodium 960 mg, Fiber 3 g

U.S. Diabetic exchanges per serving: 1 starch, 3 medium-fat meat, 6 fat (1 carb)

CHEF'S CORNER

Though there are variations, *gremolata* is an Italian flavor combination traditionally consisting of finely grated lemon zest, garlic and fresh Italian parsley.

Mascarpone is a fresh and very rich cow's milk cheese from Italy. Cream cheese can be substituted for mascarpone, if desired.

23 minutes

BEEF ENCHILADA CASSEROLE

To speed up this family-pleasing dish, the ground beef mixture is cooked on the stovetop, then the whole casserole is heated in the microwave. No oven is required!

1 lb (500 g) 95% lean ground beef

1 tbsp (15 mL) **Southwestern Seasoning Mix**

1/4 tsp (1 mL) salt

1 can (10 oz/295 mL) enchilada sauce

3/4 cup (75 mL) water

1/2 cup (125 mL) medium thick and chunky salsa

12 (6-in./15-cm) yellow corn tortillas

1/4 cup (50 mL) snipped fresh cilantro, divided

1 cup (250 mL) shredded Colby & Monterey Jack cheese blend, divided

Sour cream and lime wedges (optional)

1. Combine beef, seasoning mix and salt in **(10-in./25-cm) Skillet**; cook over medium-high heat 8-10 minutes or until beef is no longer pink, breaking beef into crumbles using **Mix 'N Chop**. Add enchilada sauce, water and salsa to Skillet. Bring to a simmer and remove from heat.

2. As beef mixture cooks, place tortillas in a stack and cut into 1-in. (2.5-cm) pieces using **Pizza Cutter**. Snip cilantro using **Kitchen Shears**.

3. Arrange half of the tortillas evenly over bottom of **Deep Dish Baker**; top with half of the beef mixture and half of the cheese. Sprinkle 2 tbsp (30 mL) of the cilantro over cheese. Top with remaining tortillas, beef mixture and cheese.

4. Microwave baker on HIGH 3-5 minutes or until cheese is melted. Garnish with remaining 2 tbsp (30 mL) cilantro. Serve with sour cream and lime wedges, if desired.

Yield: 6 servings

U.S. Nutrients per serving: Calories 340, Total Fat 14 g, Saturated Fat 6 g, Cholesterol 65 mg, Carbohydrate 33 g, Protein 24 g, Sodium 750 mg, Fiber 6 g

U.S. Diabetic exchanges per serving: 2 starch, 2½ medium-fat meat (2 carb)

CHEF'S CORNER
Easily cut a stack of tortillas using Pizza Cutter.

If desired, 1 tbsp (15 mL) taco seasoning mix can be substituted for the Southwestern Seasoning Mix.

For a variation in flavor, substitute ground turkey and green enchilada sauce for the beef and red enchilada sauce, if desired.

For a spicier kick, hot salsa can be substituted for medium salsa, if desired.

If yellow corn tortillas are not available, white corn tortillas can be substituted.

21 minutes

CHIPOTLE-HERB FLANK STEAK WITH CILANTRO RICE

A smoky compound butter and flavorful rice come together quickly while the steak is grilled.

STEAK

- 1 lb (500 g) beef flank steak
- 1 tbsp (15 mL) vegetable oil
- Salt and coarsely ground black pepper

CILANTRO RICE

- 1 cup (250 mL) uncooked long grain white rice
- ¼ cup (50 mL) chopped fresh cilantro
- 4 oz (125 g) queso fresco

CHIPOTLE-HERB BUTTER

- 1 chipotle pepper in adobo sauce and 1 tbsp (15 mL) adobo sauce
- 1 lime
- 1 tbsp (15 mL) finely chopped fresh cilantro
- ¼ cup (50 mL) butter, softened

CHEF'S CORNER

Compound butters like chipotle-herb butter add a touch of sophistication to everyday meals. Besides flavoring meat, they also enhance the flavor of grilled fish or steamed vegetables. Bring the butter to room temperature before combining with other ingredients.

This chipotle-herb butter recipe can be easily doubled and frozen for another use.

Leftover chipotle peppers can be stored in the freezer. Place chipotle peppers in a single layer in a resealable plastic freezer bag. When a recipe calls for chipotle peppers, simply break off the number of peppers you need.

1. Preheat oven to 350°F (180°C). For steak, heat **Grill Pan** over medium-high heat 5 minutes. Brush both sides of steak with oil and season with salt and black pepper. Place steak into pan; top with **Grill Press**. Cook steak 4 minutes on each side or until grill marks appear.

2. Remove press and place pan into oven; roast 5-7 minutes or until **Pocket Thermometer** registers 140°F (60°C) for medium-rare doneness. Carefully remove pan from oven using **Oven Mitts**; transfer steak to plate and let stand 5 minutes (temperature will rise to 145°F/63°C).

3. As steak cooks, start rice. Cook rice according to package directions using **(2-qt./2-L) Saucepan**. Meanwhile, chop all cilantro; set aside ¼ cup (50 mL) for rice.

4. To start butter, remove seeds from chipotle pepper with **Paring Knife**; finely chop using **Food Chopper**. Juice lime to measure 1½ tsp (7 mL) juice. Combine chipotle pepper, adobo sauce, remaining 1 tbsp (15 mL) cilantro, lime juice and butter in **Prep Bowl**; mix well.

5. To finish rice, crumble queso fresco over rice; stir in reserved cilantro.

6. To serve, microwave butter on HIGH 20 seconds or until melted. Transfer steak to cutting board; carve diagonally against the grain into thin slices using **Carving Set**. Transfer sliced steak to serving plates, drizzle with melted butter and serve with rice.

Yield: 4 servings

U.S. Nutrients per serving: Calories 530, Total Fat 26 g, Saturated Fat 12 g, Cholesterol 80 mg, Carbohydrate 40 g, Protein 31 g, Sodium 310 mg, Fiber less than 1 g

U.S. Diabetic exchanges per serving: 2½ starch, 3 medium-fat meat, 2 fat (2½ carb)

29 minutes

PORK TENDERLOIN TACOS

These easy-to-prepare tacos give you all of the spice and flavor of chorizo without all of the fat.

1 medium onion	1 tsp (5 mL) salt
½ cup (125 mL) snipped fresh cilantro	8 (6-in./15-cm) corn tortillas
1 pork tenderloin (about 1 lb/500 g)	¼ cup (50 mL) red wine vinegar
2 tsp (10 mL) vegetable oil	Salsa, diced avocados, chopped onion,
3 garlic cloves, pressed	lime wedges and sour cream
2 tbsp (30 mL) chili powder	(optional)

1. Coarsely dice onion using **Santoku Knife**. Snip cilantro using **Kitchen Shears**; set onion and cilantro aside.

2. To start pork, trim fat and silver skin from pork tenderloin using **Boning Knife**. Slice pork lengthwise into long, thin strips and then crosswise into small pieces; place into **Small Batter Bowl**. Add oil, garlic, chili powder and salt; mix well.

3. To warm tortillas, place four of the tortillas into **(12-in./30-cm) Skillet**; heat over medium heat 1 minute on each side or until warm. Repeat with remaining tortillas; set aside and keep warm.

4. Increase heat to medium-high; lightly spray same Skillet with vegetable oil using **Kitchen Spritzer**. To start cooking pork, add half of the pork to Skillet and cook undisturbed 2 minutes or until browned; remove from Skillet and keep warm. Repeat with remaining pork.

5. Add onion and vinegar to Skillet and cook 2 minutes, stirring often with **Spoon**. Return pork to Skillet; cook 2-3 minutes or until pork is cooked through.

6. To serve, spoon pork mixture into tortillas and sprinkle with cilantro; fold tortillas over. Serve with salsa, diced avocados, chopped onion, lime wedges and sour cream, if desired.

Yield: 4 servings

Light • U.S. Nutrients per serving: Calories 300, Total Fat 8 g, Saturated Fat 2 g, Cholesterol 75 mg, Carbohydrate 30 g, Protein 28 g, Sodium 760 mg, Fiber 5 g

U.S. Diabetic exchanges per serving: 1½ starch, 3 low-fat meat (1½ carb)

CHEF'S CORNER

Quickly slice pork by cutting the tenderloin lengthwise into long, thin strips, then cutting the strips crosswise into small pieces, about 2 in. x 1 in. (5 cm x 2.5 cm). For optimal browning and rich flavor, cook pork in two batches. Overcrowding the Skillet will steam rather than brown the meat.

To remove silver skin from pork tenderloin, insert the blade of Boning Knife underneath the silver skin, keeping the blade angled away from the meat as you cut along the entire length of the silver skin.

Place heated tortillas into **Large Micro-Cooker®** to keep warm. If necessary, you can re-heat them quickly in the microwave on HIGH for 30 seconds.

28 minutes

BROWN BUTTER TORTELLINI WITH SPINACH & HAM

This simple pasta toss uses the method of draining the tortellini right over fresh spinach leaves to quickly wilt the spinach with the pasta cooking water.

1 pkg (20 oz or 700 g) refrigerated cheese-filled tortellini

1 pkg (6 oz/175 g) fresh baby spinach leaves (about 8 cups/2 L)

1 8-oz (250-g) piece cooked ham steak

1 large red bell pepper

¼ cup (50 mL) butter (do not substitute margarine)

Coarsely ground black pepper (optional)

1. To cook tortellini, bring salted water to a boil in **(4-qt./4-L) Casserole**; add tortellini and cook according to package directions.

2. As tortellini cook, place spinach into large **Colander**. Dice ham with **Santoku Knife**. Finely dice bell pepper. Drain tortellini over spinach in Colander.

3. Add butter to **(12-in./30-cm) Skillet**; heat over medium heat 5-7 minutes or until butter is a deep brown color, occasionally swirling Skillet. Immediately add bell pepper. Reduce heat to low; add ham, tortellini and spinach. Gently toss to coat with **Bamboo Spatulas**.

4. To serve, spoon tortellini mixture onto serving plates. Sprinkle with black pepper, if desired.

Yield: 6 servings

U.S. Nutrients per serving: Calories 380, Total Fat 13 g, Saturated Fat 7 g, Cholesterol 65 mg, Carbohydrate 48 g, Protein 19 g, Sodium 1050 mg, Fiber 5 g

U.S. Diabetic exchanges per serving: 3 starch, 2 medium-fat meat (3 carb)

CHEF'S CORNER

Getting the butter to brown evenly is easy if you melt the butter over moderate heat and swirl the pan occasionally. Adding finely diced red bell pepper to the butter as soon as it reaches a deep brown color cools the butter and prevents burning, preserving the delicate, nutty flavor.

A ham steak is a great way to savor all the flavor of a traditional bone-in ham without buying a whole ham. Ham steaks come from the center of the ham and are 94% lean, the leanest part of the ham.

Ravioli can be substituted for the tortellini, if desired.

Diced cooked chicken can be substituted for the ham, if desired.

27 minutes

TUSCAN WHITE BEAN AND SAUSAGE STEW

Traditionally, this hearty stew would start a day in advance with soaking beans overnight. Using canned beans and tomatoes speeds up this recipe considerably.

³/₄ lb (350 g) hot Italian sausage links	2 cups (500 mL) chicken broth
2 medium carrots	4 garlic cloves, pressed
1 medium bulb fresh fennel	2 cans (15 oz or 540 mL each) cannellini beans
1 can (14.5 oz or 398 mL) petite diced tomatoes, undrained	1 pkg (18 g) fresh basil

1. Remove casings from sausage. Cut in half lengthwise, then cut crosswise into ¹/₂-in. (1-cm) nuggets (see Chef's Corner).

2. Place sausage into (4-qt./4-L) Casserole and cook over medium heat 5 minutes or until golden brown, stirring occasionally with Bamboo Spoon.

3. As sausage cooks, peel carrots. Chop carrots and fennel with Santoku Knife; add to Casserole and cook an additional 3-5 minutes or until sausage is no longer pink and vegetables begin to brown.

4. Stir tomatoes, broth and garlic into sausage mixture. Drain and rinse beans using small Colander; add to Casserole.

5. Simmer stew, uncovered, 10-12 minutes or until vegetables are tender. As stew simmers, chop basil. Remove Casserole from heat; stir in basil. Serve immediately.

Yield: 6 servings

U.S. Nutrients per serving (1 cup/250 mL): Calories 330, Total Fat 18 g, Saturated Fat 7 g, Cholesterol 45 mg, Carbohydrate 27 g, Protein 16 g, Sodium 800 mg, Fiber 7 g

U.S. Diabetic exchanges per serving (1 cup/250 mL): 1 starch, 2 high-fat meat, ¹/₂ fat (1 carb)

CHEF'S CORNER

To quickly and evenly cook sausage, it is helpful to cut it into nuggets. The nuggets also give the stew a more "finished" look. First, remove the casings using Boning Knife. Then, cut sausages in half lengthwise and then crosswise into ¹/₂-in. (1-cm) nuggets.

Fresh fennel, a fast flavor-booster in quick recipes like this one, gives this stew a subtle anise flavor. Fennel is widely used in Italian and French dishes. To chop fennel, remove stalks and root end, cut out core and chop into cubes. The lacy fronds can also be used as a garnish.

Diced onion can be substituted for the fennel, if desired.

29 minutes

JERK PORK TENDERLOIN WITH MANGO SALAD

The pork is seared on the stovetop and finished in the oven while the salad is prepared for a sweet and spicy combination.

PORK

- 2 tsp (10 mL) vegetable oil
- 1 lb (500 g) pork tenderloin
- 1 tbsp (15 mL) **Jamaican Jerk Rub**

MANGO SALAD

- 2 green onions with tops, divided
- 1 small red bell pepper
- 2 large mangoes
- 1 lime
- 1 tsp (5 mL) Jamaican Jerk Rub

1. Preheat oven to 350°F (180°C). For pork, add oil to **(10-in./25-cm) Sauté Pan**; heat over medium-high heat 1-3 minutes or until shimmering. As pan heats, trim fat and silver skin from pork tenderloin and cut pork in half crosswise using **Boning Knife**.

2. Coat pork with jerk rub. Cook 3-5 minutes or until browned on all sides, turning occasionally. Transfer pan to oven and roast 12-15 minutes or until **Pocket Thermometer** registers 155°F (68°C) for medium doneness. Carefully remove pan from oven using **Oven Mitts**; transfer pork to plate. Tent with foil and let stand 5 minutes (temperature will rise to 160°F/71°C).

3. As pork roasts, start salad. Thinly slice green onions on a bias using **Chef's Knife**. Set aside 1 tbsp (15 mL) of the tops for garnish. Place remaining green onions into **Classic Batter Bowl**. Peel bell pepper using **Serrated Peeler**. Slice off top and bottom of pepper; discard or reserve for another use. Remove and discard seeds and ribs from sides of pepper; slice into thin julienne strips.

4. To finish salad, peel and slice mangoes (see Chef's Corner). Juice lime using **Citrus Press** to measure 1 tbsp (15 mL) juice. Add pepper strips, mango slices, lime juice and remaining 1 tsp (5 mL) jerk rub to batter bowl; toss thoroughly.

5. To serve, slice pork crosswise into medallions and serve with salad. Garnish with reserved green onion tops.

Yield: 4 servings

Light • U.S. Nutrients per serving: Calories 230, Total Fat 7 g, Saturated Fat 1.5 g, Cholesterol 75 mg, Carbohydrate 19 g, Protein 24 g, Sodium 260 mg, Fiber 2 g

U.S. Diabetic exchanges per serving: 1 fruit, 3 low-fat meat (1 carb)

CHEF'S CORNER

For a pleasantly tender texture that complements the mango slices, the bell pepper is first peeled using the Serrated Peeler before slicing into thin strips. Removing the ribs from the pepper gives it a professional, finished look.

To slice a mango, use **Utility Knife** to cut thin slices from both ends of the fruit. Stand fruit upright, wide end down, on cutting board. Slice off peel from top to bottom. Slice flesh alongside the large, flat pit. Lay mango flesh down on cutting board and slice into 1/4-in. (6-mm) slices.

Jarred mangoes, found in the refrigerated produce section of most grocery stores, can be substituted for the fresh mangoes, if desired.

28 minutes

lopt

KOREAN-STYLE BEEF BOWL

For maximum flavor in minimum time, marinate small pieces of skirt steak in this sweet and spicy marinade while the rice is cooking.

STEAK AND MARINADE

- 2 green onions with tops, divided
- 1 lb (500 g) skirt steak
- 2 garlic cloves, pressed
- 3 tbsp (45 mL) soy sauce
- 1 tbsp (15 mL) sesame oil
- 1 tsp (5 mL) coarsely ground black pepper
- 1 tbsp (15 mL) sugar
- 1 tsp (5 mL) vegetable oil

RICE AND VEGETABLES

- 1 cup (250 mL) uncooked jasmine rice
- 2 medium carrots
- 2 cups (500 mL) bean sprouts

1. For steak and marinade, thinly slice green onions using **Santoku Knife**, reserving 1 tbsp (15 mL) of the tops for garnish; place remaining green onions into **Classic Batter Bowl**.

2. Cut steak crosswise into 2-in. (5-cm) pieces. Slice each piece into thin strips, cutting against the grain (see Chef's Corner); add to batter bowl. Press garlic over beef. Add soy sauce, sesame oil, black pepper and sugar; mix well. Cover and refrigerate until ready to use.

3. As beef marinates, microwave rice according to package directions using **Rice Cooker Plus**.

4. Meanwhile, for vegetables, peel carrots; discard skin. Continue peeling carrots to make long ribbons. Place ribbons into ice water until ready to serve.

5. To finish steak, add vegetable oil to **(12-in./30-cm) Skillet**; heat over medium-high heat 1-3 minutes or until shimmering. Add beef to Skillet in a single layer and cook undisturbed 2 minutes or until beef is brown. Stir; cook an additional 3-4 minutes or until beef is no longer pink. Remove from heat.

6. Remove rice from microwave and fluff with a fork. To serve, divide rice among serving bowls and serve with beef, carrots and bean sprouts. Garnish with reserved green onion tops.

Yield: 4 servings

U.S. Nutrients per serving: Calories 410, Total Fat 20 g, Saturated Fat 7 g, Cholesterol 70 mg, Carbohydrate 29 g, Protein 28 g, Sodium 790 mg, Fiber 2 g

U.S. Diabetic exchanges per serving: 2 starch, 3 medium-fat meat, ½ fat (2 carb)

CHEF'S CORNER

Skirt steak is a flavorful, boneless cut from the beef flank and should always be sliced against the grain, or it can be tough. The grain of the meat is the direction that the fibers of the muscle run. Skirt steak looks like a long belt of meat with the grain running crosswise. By cutting the strip of meat into short sections, you can easily slice against the grain for the most tender results.

If desired, serve this dish with *kim chee*, a spicy and garlicky Korean condiment made with pickled cabbage.

29 minutes

TOASTED ANGEL HAIR WITH SAUSAGE & PEPPERS

This attractive pasta dish is packed with flavor by toasting angel hair pasta and then simmering it with peppers, garlic and fresh basil.

- 1 lb (500 g) bulk hot Italian sausage
- 2 medium red bell peppers
- 1 lb (500 g) uncooked angel hair pasta
- 3 garlic cloves, pressed
- 5¼ cups (1.24 L) reduced-sodium chicken broth
- 1 cup (250 mL) fresh basil, divided
- 1 oz (30 g) Parmesan cheese

1. Place sausage into **(12-in./30-cm) Skillet**. Cook over medium heat 8-10 minutes or until no longer pink, breaking into crumbles with **Mix 'N Chop**; remove sausage from Skillet and set aside.

2. As sausage cooks, slice off tops and bottoms of bell peppers; remove and discard seeds and stems. Finely chop tops and bottoms using **Food Chopper**. Remove and discard seeds and ribs from sides of peppers; slice into thin julienne strips.

3. Add pasta to Skillet and toast 8-10 minutes, stirring after each 2-minute interval with **Chef's Tongs**. Press garlic over pasta and add broth, all of the peppers and cooked sausage. Bring to a boil; cover, reduce heat and simmer vigorously 5-6 minutes or until pasta is tender.

4. As pasta simmers, chop basil, reserving half for garnish. When pasta is tender, remove from heat and stir in remaining basil.

5. To serve, divide pasta mixture among serving bowls; grate cheese over pasta using **Deluxe Cheese Grater**. Garnish with reserved basil.

Yield: 8 servings

U.S. Nutrients per serving: Calories 430, Total Fat 20 g, Saturated Fat 7 g, Cholesterol 45 mg, Carbohydrate 45 g, Protein 20 g, Sodium 840 mg, Fiber 3 g

U.S. Diabetic exchanges per serving: 3 starch, 1½ high-fat meat, 1 fat (3 carb)

CHEF'S CORNER

Toasting the pasta provides a nutty flavor and an interesting color contrast. Toasting the pasta in the same pan as the sausage imparts flavor from the sausage to the pasta.

Heat broth in microwave or in a separate saucepan to cut down on the time it takes for the pasta to come to a boil.

26 minutes

SPP

ITALIAN MEATBALL SOUP

This quick soup starts with prepared meatballs that are simmered in a hearty tomato broth.

2 medium carrots
2 stalks celery
1 small onion
2 tbsp (30 mL) tomato paste
4 garlic cloves, pressed
1 tbsp (15 mL) **Italian Seasoning Mix**
1 can (28 oz or 796 mL) crushed tomatoes in puree

2 cups (500 mL) beef broth
1½ cups (375 mL) water
16 frozen fully cooked meatballs (about ½ oz/15 g each)
Salt and coarsely ground black pepper
Ciabatta Croutons (optional, see Chef's Corner)

1. Peel carrots with **Vegetable Peeler**. Finely chop carrots, celery and onion with **Food Chopper**.

2. Lightly spray **(4-qt./4-L) Casserole** with oil and add carrots, celery and onion. Cook over medium heat 4-5 minutes or until vegetables begin to brown, stirring occasionally.

3. Push vegetables to one side of Casserole. Add tomato paste; cook and stir 1-2 minutes or until tomato paste begins to caramelize.

4. Add pressed garlic and seasoning mix; mix well. Stir in tomatoes, broth and water; bring to a simmer.

5. Cut meatballs in half using **Chef's Knife**; add to soup. Simmer an additional 10-12 minutes; season to taste with salt and black pepper. Serve hot and garnish with Ciabatta Croutons, if desired.

Yield: 4 servings

Light • U.S. Nutrients per serving: Calories 230, Total Fat 8 g, Saturated Fat 2.5 g, Cholesterol 45 mg, Carbohydrate 26 g, Protein 15 g, Sodium 900 mg, Fiber 6 g

U.S. Diabetic exchanges per serving: 1 starch, 2 medium-fat meat (1 carb)

CHEF'S CORNER
Finely chopped vegetables allow for better distribution of flavor. As the vegetables finish cooking, the tomato paste is caramelized, adding a deep, rich flavor to the soup.

To make Ciabatta Croutons, preheat oven to 425°F (220°C). Slice one 6-oz (175-g) ciabatta loaf or other crusty Italian bread into 1-in. (2.5-cm) cubes using **Bread Knife** (about 3 cups/750 mL cubes). Toss bread cubes with 1 tbsp (15 mL) olive oil and arrange in an even layer on **Large Bar Pan**. Bake 12-14 minutes or until golden brown.

27 minutes

MOROCCAN PORK CHOPS

This pork dish features a balsamic reduction with a traditional combination of green olives, capers and raisins for an enticing salty-sweet flavor.

SAUCE

- ½ cup (125 mL) white balsamic vinegar
- ¼ cup (50 mL) raisins
- 2 shallots
- ¼ cup (50 mL) pimento-stuffed green olives
- ¼ cup (50 mL) packed brown sugar
- 2 tbsp (30 mL) capers

RICE

- 1½ cups (375 mL) water
- ½ tsp (2 mL) salt
- 1 cup (250 mL) uncooked basmati rice
- 2 tbsp (30 mL) snipped fresh parsley

PORK

- 4 boneless pork loin chops, cut ½ in. (1 cm) thick (4-6 oz/125-175 g each)
- ½ tsp (2 mL) salt
- ¼ tsp (1 mL) coarsely ground black pepper
- 2 tbsp (30 mL) all-purpose flour
- 2 tbsp (30 mL) olive oil

CHEF'S CORNER

Seasoning the pork with salt and black pepper before dredging in flour seals in flavor.

Soaking the raisins rehydrates them prior to cooking, making them plump and juicy.

White balsamic vinegar is made with white wine and is aged in the same way as regular balsamic vinegar. Regular balsamic vinegar can be substituted for the white, if desired.

1. To start sauce, pour vinegar into **Prep Bowl**; microwave on HIGH 1 minute. Add raisins; set aside to soak. To start rice, combine water and salt in **(1.5-qt/1.5-L) Saucepan**; bring to a boil. Add rice; cover and simmer over low heat 15 minutes or until water is absorbed. Remove from heat.

2. For pork, season pork with salt and black pepper. Dredge in flour, shaking off excess. Add oil to **(10-in./25-cm) Skillet**; heat over medium-high heat 1-3 minutes or until shimmering. Add pork; cook 2-3 minutes on each side or until golden brown. Remove from Skillet.

3. Meanwhile, to finish sauce, chop shallots and olives using **Food Chopper**. Reduce heat to medium. Add shallots to Skillet; cook and stir until golden. Add raisin mixture; simmer 1 minute or until liquid is slightly reduced. Stir in olives, sugar and capers. Simmer 2 minutes or until sauce starts to thicken.

4. Add pork chops to sauce; simmer gently 3-5 minutes or internal temperature reaches 155°F (68°C), turning pork chops to coat well with sauce. Remove from heat (temperature will rise to 160°F/71°C).

5. To serve, snip parsley using **Kitchen Shears**. Stir parsley into rice. Divide rice among serving plates; top with pork and sauce.

Yield: 4 servings

Light • U.S. Nutrients per serving: Calories 560, Total Fat 16 g, Saturated Fat 3.5 g, Cholesterol 65 mg, Carbohydrate 75 g, Protein 29 g, Sodium 1060 mg, Fiber 2 g

U.S. Diabetic exchanges per serving: 2 starch, 3 fruit, 3 medium-fat meat (5 carb)

20 minutes

meatless

Crunchy Breakfast Tacos, p. 119

SPANISH-STYLE STUFFED PEPPERS

Packaged saffron rice gives these stuffed peppers fabulous flavor. Steaming these peppers in the microwave makes this recipe even faster to prepare.

1 pkg (5 oz or 175 g) yellow saffron rice (plus ingredients to make rice)	¼ cup (50 mL) chopped fresh cilantro, divided
2 medium red bell peppers	1 tsp (5 mL) olive oil
2 medium tomatoes	2 garlic cloves, pressed
1 poblano pepper or small green bell pepper	¾ cup (75 mL) shredded Mexican cheese blend, divided
1 green onion with top	2 tbsp (30 mL) water

1. Prepare rice according to package directions in **(1.5-qt./1.5-L) Saucepan**.

2. As rice cooks, prepare bell peppers. Slice bell peppers in half lengthwise; remove and discard stems and seeds. Microwave, covered, in **Large Micro-Cooker®** on HIGH 3-4 minutes or until crisp-tender. Carefully remove bell peppers and pat dry with paper towels.

3. Meanwhile, core tomatoes and scoop out seeds with **Core & More**. Using **Santoku Knife**, dice tomatoes and poblano pepper. Slice green onion. Chop cilantro.

4. Add oil to **(10-in./25-cm) Skillet**; heat over medium heat 1-3 minutes or until shimmering. Add tomatoes, poblano pepper, green onion, half of the cilantro and pressed garlic; cook 2-3 minutes or until onion is tender.

5. Stir vegetable mixture into rice in Saucepan; add ½ cup (125 mL) of the cheese. Place bell peppers cut side up into Skillet; spoon rice mixture evenly into each pepper and sprinkle with remaining cheese. Add water to Skillet. Cover Skillet and heat over medium-low heat 3-5 minutes or until cheese is melted. Sprinkle with remaining cilantro.

Yield: 4 servings

Light • U.S. Nutrients per serving: Calories 240, Total Fat 8 g, Saturated Fat 4.5 g, Cholesterol 20 mg, Carbohydrate 35 g, Protein 9 g, Sodium 620 mg, Fiber 2 g

U.S. Diabetic exchanges per serving: 2 starch, 1 vegetable, 1½ fat (2 carb)

CHEF'S CORNER
We used packaged yellow saffron rice, available in most grocery stores, to save time in preparing this recipe. Yellow rice is flavored with onion and garlic as well as saffron, the most expensive spice in the world. Saffron adds a unique flavor and a beautiful color to the rice.

For a heartier main dish, add 6 oz (175 g) cooked chorizo sausage to the rice mixture, if desired.

29 minutes

CAPRESE PIZZAS

Refrigerated pizza dough gives you a head start on this Italian classic. The dough is cut into three long strips for a dramatic presentation.

TOPPINGS

   3 medium vine-ripened tomatoes

   1 tsp (5 mL) salt

   2 tbsp (30 mL) chopped fresh basil

   1 tbsp (15 mL) **Basil Oil** or olive oil

   8 oz (250 g) fresh mozzarella cheese

      Coarsely ground black pepper

CRUSTS

   1 tsp plus 1 tbsp (5 mL plus 15 mL) Basil Oil or olive oil, divided

   1 package (13.8 oz or 283 g) refrigerated pizza crust

   1 garlic clove, pressed

   1 oz (30 g) Parmesan cheese

1. Preheat oven to 425°F (220°C). For toppings, slice tomatoes into ¼-in. (6-mm) slices. Place onto paper towel-lined cutting board. Sprinkle both sides evenly with salt; let stand 15 minutes.

2. Meanwhile, for crusts, lightly brush **Rectangle Stone** with 1 tsp (5 mL) of the oil. Unroll dough onto baking stone. Press garlic into **Prep Bowl** and combine with remaining 1 tbsp (15 mL) oil; brush over dough. Grate Parmesan cheese using **Deluxe Cheese Grater** fitted with coarse grating drum; sprinkle evenly over dough.

3. Cut dough lengthwise into thirds with **Pizza Cutter**. Carefully move dough strips slightly apart on baking stone. Bake 11-12 minutes or until bottom of crusts are light golden brown.

4. While crusts bake, finish toppings. Chop basil using **Santoku Knife** (see Chef's Corner); combine with oil in another Prep Bowl and set aside for later use.

5. Blot tops of tomato slices with paper towels. Slice mozzarella cheese into ¼-in.-thick (6-mm) slices. Arrange tomato and cheese slices in overlapping rows on baked crusts. Return to oven; bake an additional 4-5 minutes or just until cheese melts.

6. Remove baking stone from oven. To serve, brush basil mixture over pizzas using **Chef's Silicone Basting Brush** and sprinkle with black pepper.

Yield: 6 servings

U.S. Nutrients per serving: Calories 350, Total Fat 17 g, Saturated Fat 7 g, Cholesterol 35 mg, Carbohydrate 35 g, Protein 15 g, Sodium 950 mg, Fiber 2 g

U.S. Diabetic exchanges per serving: 2 starch, 1 vegetable, 1 high-fat meat, 1½ fat (2 carb)

CHEF'S CORNER

Salting tomatoes pulls out the excess moisture, preventing a soggy pizza. Blotting well with paper towels results in a more concentrated flavor.

To easily chop basil, stack leaves on top of each other and roll into a tight cylinder. Slice crosswise to form ribbons. Turn basil ribbons and slice crosswise again.

29 minutes

HOT & SOUR SOUP

Red curry paste and dried shiitake mushrooms deliver authentic flavor.

6 cups (1.5 L) chicken broth, divided
4 dried shiitake mushrooms
3 green onions with tops
¼ cup (50 mL) rice vinegar
¼ cup (50 mL) reduced-sodium soy sauce

1-2 tsp (5-10 mL) Thai red curry paste
2 medium carrots
3 tbsp (45 mL) cornstarch
¼ cup (50 mL) water
1 pkg (14 oz or 350 g) tofu
   (see Chef's Corner)
3 eggs

1. To soak mushrooms, pour ½ cup (125 mL) of the broth into **Prep Bowl**; microwave on HIGH 30-60 seconds or until boiling. Add mushrooms; let stand 10 minutes. Remove mushrooms from broth and thinly slice; set aside with broth.

2. As mushrooms soak, slice green onions; set tops aside for garnish. Lightly spray **(4-qt./4-L) Casserole** with oil using **Kitchen Spritzer**. Heat over medium-high heat 1-3 minutes or until hot. Add white parts of onions; cook and stir 1 minute or until tender. Add remaining broth, vinegar, soy sauce, curry paste and mushroom mixture. Cover and bring to a boil.

3. Meanwhile, peel carrots; cut into short julienne strips using **Julienne Peeler**. Add carrots to soup; reduce to a simmer and cook 5 minutes.

4. Whisk cornstarch with water in Prep Bowl. Whisk into soup; simmer 5 minutes. Meanwhile, drain tofu and cut into ½-in. (1-cm) cubes; add to soup.

5. Turn off heat. Lightly beat eggs in **Small Batter Bowl**; drizzle into soup. Cover and let stand 5 minutes or until eggs are cooked. Garnish with reserved onion tops and serve.

Yield: 6 servings (9 cups/2.1 L)

U.S. Nutrients per serving (1½ cups/375 mL): Calories 140, Total Fat 6 g, Saturated Fat 1 g, Cholesterol 105 mg, Carbohydrate 11 g, Protein 11 g, Sodium 880 mg, Fiber 1 g

U.S. Diabetic exchanges per serving (1½ cups/375 mL): 1 fruit, 1½ low-fat meat (1 carb)

CHEF'S CORNER

Tofu has a bland flavor that enables it to take on the flavor of the food it is served with. Tofu is available in a variety of textures ranging from firm to silken, which is smooth and creamy. It is low in calories and high in protein.

For a heartier soup, add diced, cooked chicken.

Shiitake mushrooms have a full-bodied, woodsy flavor. They are available dried and fresh. Fresh can be substituted without soaking.

To make this a vegan recipe, substitute vegetable broth for the chicken broth, and omit the eggs.

Thai red curry paste is a spicy blend of spices and chilies. It is available in the Asian section of most grocery stores.

28 minutes

SPICY BROCCOLI FRITTATA

This frittata starts out on the stovetop and is finished in the oven to keep it tender and moist throughout.

4 oz (125 g) cream cheese, softened

8 eggs

2 tbsp (30 mL) water

1 tbsp (15 mL) Dijon mustard

2 green onions with tops
(about ½ cup/125 mL), sliced

2 plum tomatoes

1 tbsp (15 mL) butter

½-1 tsp (2-5 mL) crushed red pepper flakes

2 cups (500 mL) broccoli florets

1 cup (250 g) shredded mozzarella
cheese, divided

1. Preheat oven to 350°F (180°C). Whisk cream cheese until smooth in **Classic Batter Bowl**; gradually add eggs, water and mustard and whisk until smooth.

2. Slice green onions into ½-in. (1-cm) pieces using the **Santoku Knife**; thinly slice tomatoes.

3. Place butter and pepper flakes into **(10-in./25-cm) Skillet**; heat over medium heat 1-2 minutes or just until pepper flakes begin to brown. Immediately add broccoli and onions; cook 1-2 minutes or until onions begin to soften.

4. Pour eggs into Skillet; cook and stir 3-4 minutes or until eggs are almost set. Top evenly with half of the cheese and tomato slices; sprinkle with remaining cheese.

5. Bake 12-15 minutes or until center of egg mixture is set but still moist and internal temperature reaches 155°F (68°C). Remove frittata from oven and let stand 5 minutes (temperature will rise to 160°/71°C). Serve immediately.

Yield: 6 servings

U.S. Nutrients per serving: Calories 240, Total Fat 18 g, Saturated Fat 9 g, Cholesterol 320 mg, Carbohydrate 4 g, Protein 16 g, Sodium 320 mg, Fiber 1 g

U.S. Diabetic exchanges per serving: 1 vegetable, 2 medium-fat meat, 1½ fat (0 carb)

CHEF'S CORNER

Cooking the red pepper flakes for a few minutes activates the natural oils in the dried pepper and brings out the spiciness.

Frittatas are a versatile anytime meal because you can use a variety of vegetables and cheeses, as well as herbs and spices to create your own distinctive dish.

Asparagus can be substituted for the broccoli, if desired.

To quickly soften cream cheese, microwave on HIGH 15-20 seconds.

29 minutes

PERSIAN CHICKPEA SALAD

This salad has a pleasingly spicy dressing offset with cool mint. Rinsing the chopped onion removes some of the "bite."

DRESSING

- 1 lemon
- 1 tbsp (15 mL) olive oil
- ½ tsp (2 mL) cinnamon
- ½ tsp (2 mL) ground cumin
- ½ tsp (2 mL) salt
- ¼ tsp (1 mL) ground cayenne pepper

SALAD

- 1 can (19 oz/540 mL) chickpeas
- ½ small red onion
- 1 4-in. (10-cm) piece seedless cucumber
- 3 plum tomatoes
- 2 tbsp (30 mL) thinly sliced fresh mint
- 2 oz (60 g) queso fresco or feta cheese
- Toasted pita bread (optional, see Chef's Corner)

1. For dressing, juice lemon to measure 3 tbsp (45 mL) juice. Whisk together lemon juice, oil, cinnamon, cumin, salt and cayenne pepper in **Classic Batter Bowl.**

2. For salad, drain and rinse chickpeas in small **Colander**. Chop onion half using **Santoku Knife** and place into **Strainer**; rinse under cold running water. Drain onion and pat dry with paper towel.

3. Chop cucumber; seed and chop tomatoes. Add chickpeas, onion, cucumber and tomatoes to dressing; toss to coat. Thinly slice mint and fold into salad.

4. Dice queso fresco. Serve each salad topped with queso fresco and toasted pita bread, if desired.

Yield: 4 servings

Light • U.S. Nutrients per serving: Calories 170, Total Fat 4 g, Saturated Fat 1 g, Cholesterol 5 mg, Carbohydrate 27 g, Protein 8 g, Sodium 610 mg, Fiber 7 g

U.S. Diabetic exchanges per serving: 1 starch, 1 vegetable, ½ medium-fat meat (1 carb)

CHEF'S CORNER

Rinsing onion under running water takes away the sharpness of raw onion. This technique is also great to use when preparing homemade salsa.

Queso fresco is a mild, fresh Mexican cheese and is similar to Persian fresh cheese called panir.

For toasted pita bread, preheat oven to 450°F (230°C). Split 5 miniature whole-wheat pita bread rounds (about 3 in./ 7.5 cm) in half horizontally, then vertically with **Tomato Knife**. Arrange pita bread in a single layer on **Large Round Stone**; bake 5-6 minutes or until lightly toasted. Remove from oven.

20 minutes

PAN-FRIED POLENTA WITH VEGETABLE MARINARA

Keep tubes of prepared polenta on hand for this hearty, meatless main dish.

COATING AND POLENTA

   2 tbsp (30 mL) all-purpose flour

   ⅛ tsp (0.5 mL) coarsely ground black
      pepper

   1 egg

   1 oz (30 g) Parmesan cheese

   ¼ cup (50 mL) dry bread crumbs

   1 lb (500 g) prepared polenta

   2 tbsp (30 mL) olive oil

   2 tbsp (30 mL) butter

      Additional grated Parmesan cheese
      (optional)

VEGETABLE MARINARA

   1 tbsp (15 mL) olive oil

   1 medium zucchini

   8 oz (250 g) sliced mushrooms

   1 cup (250 mL) marinara sauce

CHEF'S CORNER

Pre-cooked polenta, available in the ethnic section of most grocery stores in sausage-shaped tubes, saves time required for cooking and cooling. Polenta doesn't need refrigeration before opening, so it is nice to have on hand for quick and easy last-minute meals.

Polenta is a staple in northern Italy and is often served as a soft, creamy porridge made with coarsely ground cornmeal. It can also be made using less water (as seen here) and sliced.

1. For coating, combine flour and black pepper in **Coating Tray**. Lightly beat egg in second tray. Grate cheese using **Deluxe Cheese Grater** fitted with fine grating drum. Combine cheese with bread crumbs in third tray.

2. To coat polenta, slice ends off polenta to flatten ends. Slice into eight equal rounds, ¾ in. (2 cm) thick. Lightly dredge rounds in flour mixture, shaking off excess; dip into egg and then into bread crumb mixture. Set aside.

3. For marinara, add oil to **(3-qt./2.8-L) Saucepan**; heat over medium-high heat 1-3 minutes or until shimmering. Dice zucchini using **Santoku Knife**. Add zucchini and mushrooms to Saucepan. Cook 3-5 minutes or until vegetables are tender. Stir in marinara sauce; simmer 5 minutes.

4. Meanwhile, to finish polenta, place oil and butter into **(10-in./25-cm) Skillet**; heat over medium heat 1-3 minutes or until butter is foamy. Add polenta rounds to Skillet. Cook 1-2 minutes on each side or until golden brown. Remove from Skillet using **Small Slotted Turner**.

5. To serve, spoon marinara over polenta and top with additional grated Parmesan cheese, if desired.

Yield: 2 servings

U.S. Nutrients per serving: Calories 630, Total Fat 26 g, Saturated Fat 9 g, Cholesterol 130 mg, Carbohydrate 78 g, Protein 21 g, Sodium 1390 mg, Fiber 7 g

U.S. Diabetic exchanges per serving: 5 starch, 1 medium-fat meat, 3 fat (5 carb)

25 minutes

POACHED EGGS FLORENTINE

Creamed spinach is even quicker to prepare using the Micro-Cooker®. The unique croutons give this classic egg dish an elegant presentation.

CROUTONS
4 slices firm white sandwich bread
Vegetable oil

SPINACH MIXTURE
1 pkg (10 oz/300 g) frozen chopped spinach
3/4 cup (175 mL) heavy whipping cream
1/2 cup (125 g) shredded Swiss cheese

2 garlic cloves, pressed
1/2 tsp (2 mL) salt

POACHED EGGS
8 cups (2 L) water
2 tbsp (30 mL) white vinegar
8 eggs
Salt (optional)
Paprika (optional)

1. Preheat oven to 350°F (180°C). For croutons, slice crusts off bread with **Bread Knife**; discard crusts. Cut bread into 1/4-in. (6-mm) strips; arrange in a single layer on **Medium Round Stone** and lightly spray with oil using **Kitchen Spritzer**. Bake 15-20 minutes or until golden brown. Remove from oven.

2. While croutons toast, prepare spinach mixture. Microwave spinach according to package directions using **Small Micro-Cooker®**. Line large **Colander** with several paper towels, add spinach. Fold over towels and squeeze out water; remove spinach from towels and place into **(1.5-qt./1.5-L) Saucepan**. Add cream, cheese, garlic and salt; cook and stir over medium heat 4-6 minutes or until cheese is melted.

3. For eggs, bring 8 cups (2 L) water and vinegar to a boil in **(12-in./30-cm) Skillet**; reduce heat to a gentle simmer. Crack one egg into **Prep Bowl** and gently add to water; repeat with remaining eggs (see Chef's Corner). Carefully move **Skimmer** under eggs to prevent sticking; cook 3-5 minutes or according to desired doneness. Remove eggs with Skimmer to paper towel-lined plate; season with salt, if desired.

4. To serve, spoon spinach mixture evenly onto serving plates; arrange croutons around edges of spinach. Top each serving with two eggs and sprinkle with paprika, if desired.

Yield: 4 servings

U.S. Nutrients per serving: Calories 460, Total Fat 32 g, Saturated Fat 16 g, Cholesterol 500 mg, Carbohydrate 22 g, Protein 22 g, Sodium 750 mg, Fiber 2 g

U.S. Diabetic exchanges per serving: 1½ starch, 2½ medium-fat meat, 3½ fat (1½ carb)

CHEF'S CORNER

To poach eggs to even doneness, slide the first egg into the water closest to the handle (this will provide a marker for your starting point). Add the remaining eggs clockwise around the edge of the Skillet. When eggs are cooked, remove with the Skimmer in the same order for best results.

Vinegar is added to the poaching water to help the eggs keep their shape and to keep the egg whites from spreading out or becoming stringy. If desired, lemon juice can be substituted for the vinegar.

For croutons with added flavor, spray bread with **Garlic Oil** using Kitchen Spritzer before toasting.

28 minutes

LIGHTNING-FAST VEGGIE CHILI

This hearty chili is jump-started by simmering tomatoes, chili powder and garlic in the Large Micro-Cooker®.

1 can (28 oz or 796 mL) diced tomatoes, undrained
3 garlic cloves, pressed
1 tbsp (15 mL) chili powder
½ tsp (2 mL) salt
1 medium yellow squash
1 medium onion

1 medium poblano pepper
1 tsp (5 mL) olive oil, divided
3 tbsp (45 mL) tomato paste
1 can (16 oz or 450 g) chili beans in sauce, undrained
¼ cup (50 mL) chopped fresh cilantro
Shredded cheddar cheese and sour cream (optional)

1. Combine tomatoes, pressed garlic, chili powder and salt in **Large Micro-Cooker®**; microwave on HIGH 5-7 minutes or until simmering. Remove from microwave and set aside.

2. Meanwhile, seed and dice yellow squash using **Petite Paring Knife** (see Chef's Corner). Dice onion and pepper using **Santoku Knife**. Add ½ tsp (2 mL) of the oil to **(4-qt./4-L) Casserole**; heat over medium-high heat 1-3 minutes or until shimmering. Add squash; cook 1-2 minutes or until tender. Set squash aside.

3. Add remaining ½ tsp (2 mL) oil to same Casserole; cook onion and pepper 3-4 minutes or until tender. Add tomato paste and cook an additional 30 seconds or until tomato paste begins to caramelize, stirring constantly.

4. Add tomato mixture to Casserole. Reduce heat to medium-low; add beans and squash. Simmer 4-5 minutes or until chili is thickened; stirring occasionally.

5. As chili simmers, chop cilantro. Stir cilantro into chili; serve with cheese and sour cream, if desired.

Yield: 4 servings

Light • U.S. Nutrients per serving: Calories 210, Total Fat 2 g, Saturated Fat 0 g, Cholesterol 0 mg, Carbohydrate 40 g, Protein 9 g, Sodium 920 mg, Fiber 14 g

U.S. Diabetic exchanges per serving: 1½ starch, 1 vegetable (1½ carb)

CHEF'S CORNER

Remove seeds from yellow squash to avoid excess moisture in chili by cutting squash in quarters lengthwise, then removing seeds and dicing with Petite Paring Knife.

The fresh vegetables are sautéed for the best flavor, then combined with tomato mixture, which is started in the microwave for a slow-cooked taste.

Tomato paste lends depth to this dish. Allowing it to caramelize slightly enhances the flavor of the chili.

For an interesting twist, serve over multi-grain tortilla chips with shredded cheese, or use as a great topping for baked potatoes.

28 minutes

CRUNCHY BREAKFAST TACOS

Here is an interesting twist on breakfast that the whole family will enjoy. A quick blender salsa is added to eggs after they are soft-set.

TOMATILLO SALSA

- 8 oz (250 g) tomatillos (about 3 medium tomatillos), husks removed
- 1 jalapeño pepper, stemmed
- 1/4 cup (50 mL) fresh cilantro
- 1/2 tsp (2 mL) salt

TACOS

- 1/4 cup (50 mL) chopped fresh cilantro
- 1 tomato
- 8 hard taco shells
- 1 cup (250 mL) shredded Mexican cheese blend, divided
- 6 eggs
- 2 tbsp (30 mL) water
- 1 tbsp (15 mL) butter

1. Preheat oven to 350°F (180°C). For salsa, bring water to a boil in **(2-qt./1.8-L) Saucepan**. Add tomatillos and jalapeño pepper; cook 5-8 minutes or until tomatillos are tender.

2. Meanwhile, for tacos, chop cilantro and dice tomato using **Santoku Knife**; set aside.

3. To finish salsa, transfer tomatillos from Saucepan to blender container using **Slotted Spoon**. Remove jalapeño pepper from Saucepan; test for spiciness (see Chef's Corner). Add desired amount of pepper to blender; cover and blend until smooth. Add cilantro and salt; blend 2 seconds or until cilantro is coarsely chopped.

4. To finish tacos, line up taco shells, side by side, in **Medium Bar Pan**; fill with half of the cheese. Bake 5-6 minutes or until cheese is melted. Remove from oven.

5. As taco shells bake, whisk eggs and water in **Small Batter Bowl**. Place butter in **(10-in./25-cm) Skillet**; heat over medium heat 1-3 minutes or until foamy. Add eggs; cook and stir 2-3 minutes or until eggs begin to set. Add 1/4 cup (50 mL) of the salsa; cook 1-2 minutes or until eggs are completely set.

6. To serve, spoon eggs evenly into shells; sprinkle with remaining cheese, cilantro and tomato. Serve with remaining salsa.

Yield: 4 servings

U.S. Nutrients per serving: Calories 370, Total Fat 25 g, Saturated Fat 11 g, Cholesterol 350 mg, Carbohydrate 18 g, Protein 18 g, Sodium 710 mg, Fiber 3 g

U.S. Diabetic exchanges per serving: 1 starch, 2 medium-fat meat, 3 fat (1 carb)

CHEF'S CORNER

Tomatillos are also referred to as "husk tomatoes" because of their papery outer skins. Tomatillos are quite tart and are typically cooked before using. When buying tomatillos, the husks should be fresh looking, not brown and wrinkled. The fruit should be firm to the touch and not "splitting" the husk.

The heat level of jalapeño peppers can vary widely. To test for spiciness, cut off and taste the end. It's best to add the jalapeño pepper conservatively; it's far easier to spice up a mild salsa than to try to reduce the heat once too much has been added.

To save even more time in the morning, substitute prepared salsa verde for the tomatillo salsa.

25 minutes

HARVEST BROWN RICE SALAD

The slightly bitter flavor of radicchio is balanced by the sweetness of our Sweet Cinnamon Sprinkle in this colorful salad.

- 2 tbsp (30 mL) olive oil, divided
- 2 cups (500 mL) uncooked instant brown rice
- 1½ cups (375 mL) apple cider
- ½ tsp (2 mL) salt
- ⅓ cup (75 mL) sweetened dried cranberries
- 1 tbsp (15 mL) butter, melted
- 1 medium red baking apple such as Jonathan

- 2 tbsp (30 mL) **Sweet Cinnamon Sprinkle**
- 1 large head radicchio
- 5 stalks celery
- 3 tbsp (45 mL) chopped fresh chives
- ½ cup (125 mL) toasted walnuts or Cinnamon-Glazed Walnuts (see Chef's Corner)
- 2 oz (60 g) crumbled goat cheese

1. For rice mixture, add 1 tbsp (15 mL) of the oil to **(1.5-qt./1.5-L) Saucepan**; heat over medium heat 1-3 minutes or until shimmering. Add rice; stir until well coated with oil. Stir in cider and salt. Bring to a boil. Cover; reduce heat to low. Simmer 5 minutes; remove from heat. Stir in cranberries; cover and let stand 5 minutes.

2. Meanwhile, for apples, heat **Grill Pan** over medium-high heat 5 minutes. Place butter into **Prep Bowl**; microwave on HIGH 30-60 seconds or until melted. Core apple using **The Corer™**; slice crosswise into ¼-in. (6-mm) rings. Brush both sides of apple rings with butter; sprinkle with cinnamon sprinkle, gently pressing to adhere to apple.

3. Spray Grill Pan with vegetable oil using **Kitchen Spritzer**. Grill apple rings 1 minute on each side or until grill marks appear. Remove from pan. Cut six of the apple rings in half; set aside for garnish. Chop remaining apple rings into quarters; add to rice mixture.

4. Add rice mixture to **Stainless (4-qt./4-L) Mixing Bowl**; cool slightly. Set aside four large outer leaves of radicchio for later use. Thinly slice remaining radicchio using **Chef's Knife**. Thinly slice celery on a bias; chop chives. Toss vegetables and remaining 1 tbsp (15 mL) oil with rice mixture.

5. To serve, spoon salad into reserved radicchio leaves; garnish with walnuts and reserved apple. Sprinkle with crumbled goat cheese.

Yield: 4 servings

U.S. Nutrients per serving: Calories 600, Total Fat 25 g, Saturated Fat 7 g, Cholesterol 20 mg, Carbohydrate 85 g, Protein 11 g, Sodium 460 mg, Fiber 7 g

U.S. Diabetic exchanges per serving: 4 starch, 1 fruit, 1 vegetable, 4 fat (5 carb)

CHEF'S CORNER

Grilling apples intensifies the flavor and sweetness.

Cinnamon-Glazed Walnuts: Combine 2 tbsp (30 mL) Sweet Cinnamon Sprinkle, 1 tbsp (15 mL) butter, 1 tbsp (15 mL) corn syrup and ⅛ tsp (0.5 mL) salt in **(8-in./20-cm) Sauté Pan**. Stir over medium heat until butter is melted. Add 1 cup (250 mL) walnuts and cook, stirring constantly, 5-7 minutes or until walnuts are fragrant. Spread walnuts in a single layer on **Parchment Paper**. Cool completely.

If you do not have Sweet Cinnamon Sprinkle, lightly sprinkle apple rings with sugar after brushing with butter.

25 minutes

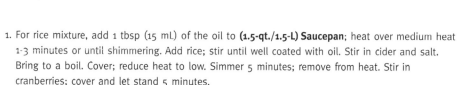

GRILLED PORTOBELLO BRUSCHETTA

This authentic Italian dish features grilled portobello mushrooms placed on grilled bread and layered with smoked mozzarella and fresh arugula.

4 slices (³⁄₄-in./2-cm thick) Vienna or
Italian bread

2 tbsp (30 mL) **Garlic Oil**

4 large portobello mushroom caps
(4-5 in./10-13 cm in diameter each)

½ cup (125 mL) light balsamic vinaigrette
salad dressing, divided

1 cup (250 mL) cherry tomatoes

6 oz (175 g) smoked mozzarella cheese
(see Chef's Corner)

4 cups (1 L) fresh arugula

1 oz (30 g) Asiago cheese

1. For bread, heat **Grill Pan** over medium heat 5 minutes. As pan heats, slice bread on a slight bias using **Bread Knife**. Brush both sides of bread with oil. Place bread onto grid of pan. Grill bread 1 minute on each side or until grill marks appear. Remove from pan and set aside.

2. As bread grills, start toppings. Brush mushrooms with 2 tbsp (30 mL) of the vinaigrette. Place mushrooms into pan. Grill 4-5 minutes on each side or until grill marks appear and mushrooms are tender. Remove from pan to cutting board.

3. As mushrooms grill, cut tomatoes into quarters; set aside. Slice mozzarella cheese into twelve ¼-in.-thick (6-mm) slices.

4. To serve, place bread onto serving plates. Place three cheese slices onto each bread slice. Slice mushrooms on a bias and arrange over cheese. Arrange tomatoes around bruschetta; drizzle tomatoes and mushrooms with ¼ cup (50 mL) of the vinaigrette. Toss arugula with remaining vinaigrette and arrange over bruschetta. Using **Vegetable Peeler**, shave Asiago cheese over arugula. Serve immediately.

Yield: 4 servings

U.S. Nutrients per serving: Calories 380, Total Fat 24 g, Saturated Fat 9 g, Cholesterol 40 mg, Carbohydrate 25 g, Protein 15 g, Sodium 810 mg, Fiber 3 g

U.S. Diabetic exchanges per serving: 1½ starch, 1 vegetable, 1 high-fat meat, 3 fat (1½ carb)

CHEF'S CORNER
Smoked mozzarella cheese infuses any dish with a distinctive smoky flavor and is a great melting cheese. Smoked mozzarella is made by cold-smoking fresh mozzarella using hardwoods, like pecan or apple, for several hours. It is then packaged in mini-loaves, slices or balls. Smoked mozzarella cheese is a great ingredient choice to add bold flavor quickly and easily.

22 minutes

BEAT THE CLOCK

Although all the recipes in this book can be prepared in under 29 minutes, below are additional time-saving tips that will allow you to trim off a few more minutes. By stocking and organizing your pantry, refrigerator and freezer, you will find yourself in control of the clock.

IN THE PANTRY

A well-stocked pantry contains the building blocks for all your recipes.

- Every month or so, stock up on pantry items that you can keep on hand.

- Create a master grocery list of staples and keep a running inventory. Examples include rice and pasta, canned tomatoes, chicken broth, condiments, spices and long-storing produce such as onions or garlic.

IN THE REFRIGERATOR

Some up-front work with fresh groceries will save you crucial time when ready to cook.

- Wash broccoli and cauliflower and cut them into florets. These will keep well for the week and can be quickly steamed or added to stir-fries or pasta dishes.

- When chopping vegetables for tonight's recipe, chop a little extra for another meal in the next few days.

- Buy pre-shredded cheeses whenever possible, with the exception of Parmesan cheese, which is much better tasting when grated fresh.

- Use pre-packaged, pre-washed produce items or foods from the supermarket's salad bar to help you with preparation.

- When a recipe calls for a half pound of cooked pasta, cook the entire box and refrigerate the rest for another day.

- Rinse bunches of fresh herbs, re-cut stems and place into a container of water. When called for in a recipe, just snip off what you need.

- If you're roasting or grilling chicken, go ahead and double the amount. It will take just about the same amount of time, and you will be ahead of the game for another night.

IN THE FREEZER

The freezer is a great place to start when you want to get ahead.

- Plan on having some easy meal-starters on hand, such as cooked ground beef, diced chicken and cooked rice. These can be thawed easily and ready to go in minutes.

- Purchase chicken breasts or chicken tenders in bulk. Dice or thinly slice them before freezing. Take them out of the freezer the night before and allow to thaw in the refrigerator all day.

- Pack foods in medium or large freezer bags and flatten as thinly as possible to make them ready for quick thawing.

- It takes the same amount of time to prepare 8 cups (2 L) of rice as it does to prepare 2 cups (500 mL). Freeze cooked rice in 1-2 cup (250-500-mL) portions. Simply reheat in the microwave when ready to use.

- Freeze leftover broth or wine in ice cube trays, then place cubes into freezer bags for quick, flavorful pan sauces.

- Chop leftover bread into crumbs and freeze for use as a crunchy topping for fish or pasta.

FOOD SAFETY AND STORAGE

When stored properly, foods stay fresher for longer periods of time, and they are ready when you are.

- When ready to use fruits and vegetables, wash well under running water.

- Cut raw fish, poultry or beef on a separate cutting board from raw vegetables or fruit to avoid cross-contamination.

- Cook foods to proper temperatures. Harmful bacteria are destroyed when food is cooked properly. Use an instant-read thermometer, and remember to wash thoroughly in hot, soapy water after each test.

- To check internal food temperatures, be sure to place the thermometer into the thickest part of foods, away from bone and/or fat.

- When cooking in a microwave oven, cover, stir and turn food for even cooking.

- Refrigerate or freeze prepared food within 2 hours.

- Wrap and label leftovers with today's date, then eat or freeze within 3 to 4 days. Check the refrigerator once a week and discard old leftovers.

- Refrigerate uncooked ground meat and poultry for only 1 or 2 days, or freeze for 3 to 4 months.

- Refrigerate cooked ground meat and poultry for 3 to 4 days, or freeze for 2 to 3 months.

RECIPE INDEX

About Our Recipes

All recipes were developed and carefully tested in The Pampered Chef® Test Kitchens. The recipes in this book have been designed to take you 29 minutes or less to prepare from start to finish, including preparation time needed for steps like chopping vegetables. The total time listed for each recipe includes all cooking, baking, cooling, chilling, standing and/or marinating time. In many cases, these steps are happening simultaneously. As an important first step, we suggest you read through the recipe and assemble the necessary ingredients and equipment. For best results, we recommend you use the ingredients indicated in the recipe.

Notes on Nutrition

The nutrition information in *29 Minutes to Dinner* can help you decide how specific recipes can fit into your overall meal plan. The nutrient values for each recipe were derived from The Food Processor, Version 8.3.0 (ESHA Research), or are provided by food manufacturers. In addition to listing calories, total fat, saturated fat, cholesterol, carbohydrate, protein, sodium and fiber, we include diabetic exchanges commonly used by people with diabetes. This information is based on the most current dietary guidelines, *Exchange Lists for Meal Planning (2003)*, by the American Diabetes Association and the American Dietetic Association. For each recipe, two lists of exchanges are provided. The first option is based on the traditional method of figuring diabetic exchanges; the second option is given in parentheses and reflects the newer system of carbohydrate counting. When using either approach to meal planning, always consult with your physician, registered dietitian or certified diabetes educator, who will address your individual needs.

Nutritional analysis for each recipe is based on the first ingredient listed whenever a choice is given and does not include optional ingredients, ingredients followed by the words "to taste," garnishes, fat used to grease pans (unless a specific amount is listed), or serving suggestions. The ingredients used in our recipes and for nutritional analyses are based on most commonly purchased foods and, unless indicated otherwise, use 2 percent reduced-fat milk and large eggs. Recipes labeled as *Light* contain 30 percent or fewer calories from fat. When salt and/or black pepper are mentioned in the ingredient list without amounts listed, nutrition information is based on an appropriate amount. When vegetable oil is called for in a recipe, nutrition information is based on canola oil.